ZACHARY MACAULAY

Zachary Macaulay

Illustration taken from Viscountess Knutsford's *Life and Letters* (1900)

ZACHARY

MACAULAY

Faith Cook

PUBLISHING WITH A MISSION

EP BOOKS
Faverdale North
Darlington, DL3 0PH,
England

e-mail: sales@epbooks.org
web: http://www.epbooks.org

First published 2012

British Library Cataloguing in Publication Data available

ISBN-13:   978-0-85234-784-3

Printed and bound in Great Britain by the MPG Books Group, Bodmin and King's Lynn.

To
my son-in-law
Chris Bennett,
kind friend and spiritual encourager

CONTENTS

LIST OF ILLUSTRATIONS

* With grateful thanks to the Evangelical Library

TIMELINE

1791	Napoleon Bonaparte First Consul of France
1793	Louis XVI of France executed. England and France at war
1794-99	Macaulay Governor of Sierra Leone
1799	Macaulay marries Selina Mills
1800	Birth of Thomas Babington Macaulay
1801	Union of Britain and Ireland
1802	William Pitt resigns — Henry Addington prime minister. Peace treaty signed with France
1803	War resumes with Napoleon
1805	Battle of Trafalgar
1806	Death of Pitt. Lord Grenville and Whigs in government
1807	Act of Abolition of Slave Trade
1814	Birth of Charles, last of Zachary and Selina's family of nine
1815	End of Napoleonic Wars with the Battle of Waterloo
1820	Death of George III
1829	Catholic Emancipation Act
1831	Death of Selina Macaulay
1832	First Reform Act
1833	Abolition of slavery — death of Wilberforce
1837	Victoria becomes Queen
1838	Death of Zachary Macaulay

INTRODUCTION

William E. Gladstone, four times prime minister of Britain, entered Parliament in 1832. Just one year later the Act finally abolishing slavery in the British Dominions was passed. Much rightful credit has been given to William Wilberforce as the moving force behind the 1807 Act that made the slave trade illegal and the build-up to the 1833 Act. But Gladstone had this to say:

> There is another name still more strongly associated with the slave question ... one who has been the unseen modest ally of Mr Wilberforce, and the pillar of his strength — a man of profound benevolence, of acute understanding, of indefatigable industry, and of that self-denying temper which is content to work in secret, to forgo the recompense of present fame, and to seek his reward beyond the grave; the name of that man is Zachary Macaulay.

This study is an attempt to look behind the scenes at this self-effacing man — one far less known than Wilberforce or his famous son, Thomas Babington Macaulay — and to correct the imbalance of the record. It is an endeavour to assess in some measure Zachary Macaulay's enormous contribution to the abolition of both the slave trade and of slavery itself in the British Dominions. More than all, as Macaulay himself would have wished, we seek to give God the glory for raising up such a man at so critical a juncture of British national history.

1

CRUMBLING FOUNDATIONS

The Macaulay household was a busy, noisy, crowded place — which is hardly surprising, for John and Margaret Macaulay had a family of twelve. John Macaulay (1720–1789), minister of Cardross Presbyterian Church, near Glasgow, and his wife often struggled to make ends meet; for not only had they to provide for the needs of a large family, but also to fund expenses incurred by visiting clergy, needy parishioners, domestic helpers and various tradesmen. For the Macaulays it was a life of continual sacrifice. But one thing troubled them more than any other: their inability to finance their children's education adequately, especially in the light of the obvious potential shown by some. And no child felt this deprivation more acutely than their third son, Zachary.

Born on 2 May 1768 during his father's first pastorate in Inveraray on the banks of Loch Fyne, western Scotland, Zachary soon began to show an unusual intelligence and a fascination with the world of books. His love of reading is the more remarkable when we learn that the child was born with sight in only one eye, a defect that had been passed down through several generations of the Macaulay forebears. Despite this handicap young Zachary nursed an early longing that one day he might be able to gain a university education. While the rest of the family was playing, working or doubtless quarrelling, Zachary could be found curled up in a corner with a book.

John Macaulay taught the children himself as much as possible, but considering the many responsibilities of his pastorate he inevitably had insufficient time to spare. And as Zachary grew older he too was expected to teach the younger members of the family. He tells us, however, with a touch of pride that he actually achieved a working knowledge of Latin, enough Greek to be able to read Homer satisfactorily, an ability to read French and a considerable grasp of mathematics. We may imagine the slim grey-eyed boy always immersed in some book whenever he had opportunity, for he had an insatiable, even obsessive passion for knowledge. Poetry, the classics, history, political developments: nothing seemed beyond his all-absorbing interests. Like many clever children, Zachary enjoyed showing off his abilities in adult company. Whenever visitors were present and some intellectual topic was raised, a childish voice would pipe up with his own contribution to the conversation — although often, as he admits, it was 'with very little judgement and a great share of conceit and assumption'. With a troubling lack of wisdom, the adults would compliment the child on his intelligence until he developed an unattractive degree of arrogance about his own opinions — a characteristic he later found hard to throw off.

Another reason why young Zachary spent so much time with his books was an accident he had at the age of nine, involving a serious break to his right arm. At least two painful operations followed, and without the aid of anaesthetics it was a traumatic experience for the boy. For the next five years he was unable to join with others in normal outdoor activities. Not until he was nearly fourteen did he recover the full use of his arm. At about the same time came the fateful day when all his long-held hopes of a university education were finally dashed. John Macaulay had to inform his son that in view of the family's financial difficulties he had no option other than to ask Zachary to leave home and earn his own living. In fact, his father had already secured a position for the boy in the finance department of a Glasgow merchant's business — a 'counting-house' as it was then called. Although Zachary fully understood his family circumstances, he was crestfallen. The hopes of years had gone. He confessed: 'I felt the disappointment very acutely and thought I lost by this arrangement all my past labours'. His cherished aspirations of academic achievement faded from that moment.

From a little child Zachary had been taught the basic truths of the Christian faith. He had enjoyed hearing sermons. We may imagine that he commented volubly on all he heard. He prayed dutifully each night, and was troubled when he acted against his conscience. But for Zachary his religion remained a notional acceptance of truths. Leaving home at only fourteen years of age, he quickly became vulnerable to the corrupting influences of some around him.

On taking up the position in Glasgow, three distinct pressures began to have an impact on Zachary's thinking and behaviour. The first sprang from his new work associates: many were coarse in their ways and indulged in excessive drinking. Although Zachary hated the taste of alcohol, he was soon joining his companions as they drank into the night. It became a mark of distinction among them to see who could drink the most before becoming totally inebriated — a competition that young Zachary contrived to win. Explaining his behaviour, he later admitted: 'I began to think excess of wine, so far from being a sin, to be a ground of glorying; and it became one of the objects of my ambition to be able to see all my companions under the table'.

Far different from such scenes was the influence of a more sophisticated company. These were the Macaulay family friends and relatives living in Glasgow at the time. Anxious that his father should not receive adverse reports of his conduct, Zachary carefully hid any signs of coarse behaviour. Among this society he copied their sophisticated ways and learnt about the most recent plays being produced and popular novels published, adding these items to his repertoire of interests. So when he had not drunk himself senseless, Zachary could be found burning the midnight oil as he devoured all the latest literature of the times.

More pernicious than the influence of heavy-drinking workmates was the company of the university students. Despite being denied a university education, Zachary sought out their society. Finding the boy highly intelligent, they welcomed him into their student social gatherings. With the Scottish Enlightenment just reaching its height, the widespread advances in science, medicine and the arts were fundamentally changing society. The student world was naturally caught up in the intellectual ferment. Coupled with this came the influence of philosophers and thinkers: men like Adam Smith, David Hume and others who downplayed and even debunked the authority of Scripture and the existence of God, truths that Zachary had long been taught to respect.

The youth proved easy prey to these rationalistic concepts. At first he recoiled with horror at the unbelief rife in the university and made some attempt to counter such arguments; but before long he gave in. Softened up by flattery and dazzled by intellectual arguments, he soon found 'every trace of religious belief' eradicated from his mind. Worse than this, he made it his aim to undermine the faith of others. In his own words he confesses: 'David Hume was now my oracle. To profane the sacred name of God, to prostitute his word to the purpose of exciting licentious merriment, to tease and perplex with questions and sarcasm, simple and well-meaning people, and to shake the faith of such of my companions as were not favoured with so bright a light as myself, was my pastime.'

Despite these spiralling downward trends, Zachary worked well and gained the respect of his superiors. But after only two years in the Glasgow merchant office a critical situation arose which once more dramatically changed the young man's life. In his account of these days Zachary remains deliberately vague in his allusions to the catalyst that brought about this change, telling us only that it resulted in an end to his career in the business. Clearly in serious trouble, he later wrote: 'The only way I could extricate myself from the labyrinth in which I was involved was [by] going abroad.' He must leave Scotland altogether. But where could he go? It has been surmised that the problem may have been some emotional entanglement with a young woman that had gone badly wrong. Certainly, in Zachary's own words, the circumstances 'led to a few sober reflections.'

A relative who had formerly been governor of Jamaica assured Zachary's father that he had excellent connections on the island and knew men of influence there who could help his son set out on the path to success and wealth. He would therefore write a number of letters of recommendation for Zachary to take with him. So in 1784, shortly before his seventeenth birthday, the young man set sail for far-off Jamaica, leaving behind all he had ever known. The long voyage gave him further space for 'sober reflections' and also time to make a number of resolutions. Two things had precipitated his downfall: his love of company — unhelpful company, as it had often proved — and the vulnerability to which an excess of alcohol can so easily expose the unwary. Zachary Macaulay resolved to keep his drinking under strict control from that moment on — a resolution from which he never deviated.

As his ship sailed into Kingston harbour and he gazed around the impressive blue bay ringed by mountains, Zachary might well have felt a pang of home-sickness. The sense of isolation rapidly worsened, as he discovered that not one of those to whom his relative had written was prepared to spare more than a passing glance at the letters of recommendation Zachary had brought. All his visions of wealth and advancement crumbled to the dust. The sixteen-year-old was utterly alone in a strange country. But a streak

of grit in Zachary's character saved him from despair, even
causing him to respond positively to a desperate situation.

Jamaica, described as 'a jewel in the English crown', had been
a British colony since 1655. The English were not slow to
spot the lucrative advantages of developing the production
of sugar cane in the island. To facilitate this, they had vastly
increased the numbers of slaves transported from the west
coast of Africa to work the plantations. At the time Zachary
stepped off the vessel carrying him to this new world of
slave-dominated labour, the slave population of Jamaica had
reached more than 200,000. Cities back in England such as
Liverpool and Bristol were developing and flourishing on
revenue secured by the lucrative profits of the slave trade
with the Caribbean.

The infamous triangular route associated with the trade
began in these English ports. Vessels were loaded with goods
for sale in Africa; on arrival these ships would dock at one
of a number of off-shore islands where black men, women
and children were being held in slave depots. Dragged from
their inland homes and villages by black tradesmen bent on
gain, or sometimes as captives from inter-tribal warfare,
these hapless prisoners would be bartered to English merchants for manufactured commodities and then crammed
mercilessly aboard the slave ships. The 'Middle Passage', as
the transatlantic voyage to the New World was called, could
take up to three months; sometimes even longer, depend-
ing on wind and storm. Kept chained together in atrocious,
stinking conditions, the slaves suffered indignity, disease
and death — a death toll that could amount to forty-five per
cent of those packed onto a single slave ship. Sharks eager

for a meal followed in the wake of the slave ships. On arrival at their destination, whether America or the West Indies, surviving slaves were sold or traded for raw materials: sugar, timber or cotton to be taken back to England.

Into this maelstrom of human exploitation Zachary Macaulay stepped in 1784 to begin life afresh after the failures of his life in Glasgow. Even though few offered him any help, it was not long before he obtained a job as a book-keeper on one of the sugar plantations. Every remnant of sensitivity in his nature recoiled at the sufferings of the slaves that he was compelled to witness. To hear the piteous cries as a weak, exhausted slave was whipped to force him to work harder appalled the young man. Worse still, his duties sometimes meant that he must carry out the punishment himself. 'My mind was at first feelingly alive to the miseries of the poor slaves. I not only revolted from the thought of myself inflicting punishment upon them, but the very sight of punishment sickened me,' he wrote to a friend.

A fearful choice lay before Zachary. Either he must write to his father begging him to send money to secure a passage home — a thing he determined he could never do in view of his family finances — or he must steel his feelings against the sufferings he was witnessing and allow his need for survival to banish pity and sensitivity. Starve or succumb: he chose the latter. Gradually he became accustomed to the crack of the whip as it lashed his fellow human beings into further servitude. Writing to the same friend from his Glasgow days, Zachary gives a vivid description of the scene: 'View me in a field of canes amidst perhaps a hundred ... cursing and bawling [slaves] while the noise of the whip resounding on their shoulders and the cries of the poor wretches would make you imagine some unlucky accident had carried you to the doleful shades.'

The 'head driver' of a gang of slaves, sometimes a black man himself, treated his underlings like a coachman dealing with a team of recalcitrant horses. Nor was this the only cruelty to which Zachary gradually became accustomed. Floggings were the order of the day for any that rebelled or refused to comply. As the slave population vastly outnumbered their white overlords, the fear of rebellions or uprisings often lay at the root of the brutal treatment meted out on the slaves.

In addition to toiling each day in the relentless heat, often in twelve-hour shifts, the slaves faced fearful risks associated with the processing of the sugar canes. As the sugar juices were squeezed from the canes in huge vertical rollers, exhausted slaves would often catch their fingers in the rollers or scald their hands in the boiling syrup as the raw sugar was refined. Many would lose fingers and even arms in horrible accidents. Under these conditions a slave's life expectancy in Jamaica could be a mere three years or less. But the abundant supply of replacement labour arriving from Africa made such statistics of little concern to the merchants and their representatives.

Describing himself as becoming 'callous and indifferent' to the suffering he was witnessing all around him, Zachary also had serious troubles of his own which he later regarded as a 'righteous retribution' for his conduct. Unaccustomed to the climate and the infectious diseases rife on the island, he experienced repeated illness. Pride and Scottish reserve prevented him from asking for help or even complaining, and the cold-hearted indifference of his associates meant that no one offered any comforts or relief. Lying on a hard floor on nothing but straw, his body wracked with fever, the young man frequently teetered on the verge of the grave. No one troubled to offer him even a drink of cold water to slake his burning thirst. The only solution was for Zachary to drag himself to some nearby stream and scoop up a little water. His own later comment describes the situation:

> I tremble to think on the stupid insensibility, nay the desperate hardiness with which at times I stood tottering on the brink of eternity. Surely, if I had died thus, my place would have been where mercy is clean gone for ever, and where even God forgets to be gracious. May I not regard myself emphatically as a brand plucked out of the burning?

As soon as he recovered, all serious thoughts quickly evaporated. Yet in spite of his surroundings, Zachary still clung to a vestige of his early training, those firm foundations laid in his home life far off in Cardross, and to his love of learning. He read poetry, cultivated his French and Latin, and studied the philosophical thoughts of the times. Amid all the coarseness of his surroundings he actually gained a reputation for culture and intelligence. In addition he learnt how to deal with ordinary men judiciously, drawing out the best from those with whom he worked. On the negative side, he also became strongly partial to the gambling table. Only his cautious Scottish thrift prevented him from squandering all his hard-earned funds.

During the next four years Zachary remained at his post in Jamaica, largely conforming to the standards around him, turning a blind eye to much of the inhumanity he witnessed. But through these experiences he was being prepared by God himself for a life work purposed for him though quite hidden as yet. Despite outward appearances, springs of compassion for the oppressed within his nature were not quite stifled by his environment and he would often plead the cause of young African boys and girls on the plantation condemned to a life of degradation and servitude.

At last in 1789 a letter came from one of his uncles, a letter telling him of 'an advantageous offer' of employment if he would consider returning home. A maze of contradictory thoughts flashed through the young man's mind. He had changed; he had become brutalized and insensitive and he knew it. What would his father[1] think of him now? Would he welcome him home? What about his favourite sister Jean to whom he had been very close? He had scarcely seen one white woman since he had arrived in Jamaica in 1784. At twenty-one years of age Zachary feared he might not know how to behave properly in feminine company. Perhaps it would be better to remain in Jamaica for life and gain a prominent position as a plantation manager. But as he weighed up the alternatives between the call of home, of family, of a job as promised by his uncle, with his present position, he decided he must venture, and at last booked a passage back to Britain.

Note

1. The lack of any mention of his mother suggests that she had died in the intervening years.

2

'PLUCKED

OUT OF THE BURNING'

Twenty-two-year-old Zachary was apprehensive at the thought of meeting his family again. Thrust into an adult world at the age of fourteen, his links with his home had been tenuous and intermittent in the intervening years. How different he was now from the raw youth who had left Scottish shores four years earlier! True, he had sailed to Jamaica in a measure of disgrace, but since then he had endured many privations, illnesses, loneliness and suffering. To survive such circumstances Zachary had become self-sufficient, independent and even callous. Worse than that, in his capacity as a plantation under-manager he had been forced to witness and often inflict grievous injustice and cruel punishment on the slave workers. As a result his emotions were crushed and brutalized, his conscience hardened.

Despite this, when he learnt on arrival that his father had just died — the father whom Zachary had respected, honoured and anticipated seeing once again — he was

stunned and dismayed. He scarcely knew what to do next.
Where should he go? Adding to his bewilderment he heard
that his favourite sister Jean, closest to him in age and
the companion of his childhood years, had left Scotland.
Following her marriage to some well-to-do country squire,
she was now living in Leicestershire in the English Midlands.
With these final threads of family life broken, little remained
to attract Zachary back to his Scottish home, particularly
after he discovered that the employment promised him by
his uncle turned out to be a mere pipe-dream.

Eventually Zachary decided to seek out his sister Jean and
her new husband, Thomas Babington. Perhaps he could stay
with them until he had decided on his future course of action.
A further shock awaited him as he caught his first glimpse
of Rothley Temple, the magnificent home where Jean now
lived. How could a girl from a poor Scottish manse have met
and married someone in such different circumstances from
herself? The story Zachary heard was fascinating. His eldest
brother, surprisingly named Aulay Macaulay, had entered
the Church of England ministry and had been appointed
vicar of a country church in Leicestershire. Not far from
his parish lay the attractive village of Rothley, surrounded
by ancient woodland known as the Charnwood Forest.
Rothley Temple stood in the heart of the village, imposing
and grand. Originally built in the thirteenth century at
the express wish of King Henry III for an order of knights
known as the Knights Templar, Rothley Temple, complete
with its own chapel, had passed into the ownership of the
Babington family at the dissolution of the monasteries in the
sixteenth century. Thomas Babington (1758–1837) was the
current owner.

Zachary's vicar brother had struck up a friendship with Thomas Babington and found him a man of earnest Christian faith. When the two decided to make a tour of the north of Scotland together — a long and arduous trek for eighteenth-century travellers — it is not surprising that Aulay wished to visit Cardross on their way north. He wanted to see any members of his family still living at home and to introduce his friend to his father. Then the unexpected happened. Thomas fell passionately in love with one of the Macaulay girls, Aulay's younger sister, Jean. Nothing could persuade him to continue with the tour until he had gained the affection of the beautiful Jean Macaulay (1763–1845) and she had agreed to marry him.

The engagement was obviously a shock for the aristocratic Babington family. Thomas's mother in particular was far from pleased. Who was this girl from an impoverished family in distant Scotland that her son was proposing to make his wife? Undaunted, Babington pressed on with arrangements for their marriage, which took place in 1787. He realized, however, that for Jean the transition from the simplicity and seclusion of a Scottish manse to the grandeur of Rothley Temple would be far from easy. Perhaps the best plan would be for her to spend a few weeks with his own sister, Mary, and her husband Thomas Gisborne (1758–1846), who lived in a nearby country estate known as Yoxall Lodge verging on the beautiful Needwood Forest in Staffordshire. It was a bold move. Thomas's own hawk-eyed mother, who had already registered her dismay over her son's choice of bride, also lived there. But the trial turned out to be a complete success.

Jean's splendid character, charm and intelligence won the old lady's heart as the younger woman quickly learnt all she needed in order to be mistress of Rothley Temple. So completely did Jean satisfy old Mrs Babington that her mother-in-law also moved to Rothley Temple to live with them and remained there until her death. Into this demanding environment young Zachary Macaulay introduced himself in 1789: uncouth, opinionated, bad-mannered and with an insufferable sense of his own superiority.

Thomas and Jean Babington welcomed the newcomer warmly, and Zachary soon discovered in Thomas qualities he admired intensely. Here was a man, upright, sincere and plain-speaking; above all a man of deep spiritual conviction and warm Christian compassion for the needs of others. And in his young brother-in-law Thomas found plenty to challenge even the most sympathetic disposition. One of Thomas and Jean's daughters long remembered hearing her parents' description of Zachary when he first came to them. He was 'thought by most people to be a disagreeable, conceited youth with self-sufficient dogmatic manners'.

From boyhood onwards Zachary had known little human love and tenderness. His conscience had been seared by the unbelief of his companions in Glasgow and much of the sensitivity of his nature blasted away by the sufferings he had been compelled to witness and inflict in the West Indies.

Almost immediately Zachary found himself drawn out in affection towards Thomas. His personal interest and concern was something Zachary had seldom known. From

his example Zachary learnt that those emotions of pity and
mercy which he had struggled to suppress in Jamaica were
not signs of weakness but were noble and right. For his part
Babington had eyes to see and admire the finer elements in
Zachary's character long suppressed by his circumstances.
As he gained Zachary's confidence, Thomas was able to
reprove some of the boorish attitudes he saw in the younger
man. Gradually he began to see an appreciable change
taking place in his whole demeanour as he responded to
the concern being shown him. 'I have never met with any
[one] who handles those wounds which sorrow makes on
the mind with such skill and tenderness as Babington,' wrote
Zachary later, and again, 'if you were aware of the extent of
my obligation to Babington, you would not be surprised that
in speaking of him I express such deep affection.'

But far above human kindness, the greatest debt which
Zachary owed to Thomas Babington was the winsome
manner in which he pointed him to Jesus Christ and to
the power of the gospel to transform his life. The Christian
grace so clearly demonstrated in Thomas and Jean moved
and melted Zachary until at last, humbled and renewed, he
too became a new man through faith in Jesus Christ. In later
years he would write:

> I never think of him [Thomas] but my thoughts are drawn
> to that Saviour with whom he first brought me acquainted,
> and if there be any consideration more than another which
> endears Babington to me it is that of the relation in which he
> stands to me in Christ. Will you wonder now that my heart
> should be melted when I think of it?

Other men, friends of Thomas Babington who visited
Rothley Temple, had also impressed Zachary deeply: men
like William Wilberforce, the politician; Henry Thornton,
the financier and philanthropist; and of course Thomas
Gisborne from Yoxall Lodge, all men who shared the same
humanitarian concerns. The Christ-like disposition which
he saw exhibited among them had been another means
of softening and moulding Zachary to the message of the
gospel which they all held and valued.

Uppermost in the conversation of Babington and his friends
whenever they met was always their social and moral
concern for the needs of others. One subject above all was
a constant theme as they spoke together: the iniquity of
the slave trade in which Britain took so prominent a part.
The bondage and humiliation that the country sanctioned
and which were so ruthlessly inflicted on their fellow men
grieved and angered them. Here was a subject about which
Zachary had first-hand knowledge — unlike Thomas and his
friends — and he was able to join in the discussions and add
some invaluable information for their consideration.

Thomas Babington was quick to appreciate that in their
ambitious campaign to abolish the slave trade they had
discovered in young Zachary Macaulay, still only twenty-
two years of age, an invaluable asset. Amazingly intelligent
and with a tireless zeal and ability for detail, he might well
be a man who could be trained and used to forward their
great cause. His four years of personal experience in Jamaica
as a book-keeper and under-manager for one of the sugar
plantations gave Zachary insight and understanding which

few of the others possessed. As yet Zachary was undecided about his future path, but unknown to him Babington had a secret agenda of his own for his brother-in-law's life and gave himself with quiet enthusiasm to shaping Zachary's thinking and vision towards that goal. But for Zachary himself as he thought back on recent years, he could only say, 'May I not regard myself emphatically as a brand plucked out of the burning?'

3

A BACKWARD GLANCE

Many distinguished-looking visitors cantered into the forecourt of Rothley Temple to call on Thomas and Jean Babington. Each was received with warmth and pleasure and, in the heavily oak-beamed sitting-room, would sit deep in conversation while Zachary Macaulay listened enthralled. Almost invariably they were discussing their endeavours to right the social ills rife in the community, and especially their attempts to awaken the national conscience to the evils of the slave trade. He would have heard of the recent death of John Thornton (1720-1790), father of Thomas Babington's close friend, Henry. John Thornton had owned extensive property adjacent to Clapham Common, three miles south-west of London, and had been one of the richest businessmen in England. But his generosity was equally startling. With the cry of the needy constantly touching his heart and purse, he had found unusual means of relief for some of society's most broken and fallen: prostitutes, debtors and aimless youths. Added to this, Zachary learnt that John Thornton had financed and settled evangelical preachers in many strategic areas throughout the country.

Two other names kept cropping up in conversations at Rothley Temple. Granville Sharp (1735-1813) had been among the first to campaign on behalf of the African slaves. In 1765, three years before Zachary was born, he had befriended a mistreated runaway slave, James Somerset, whose former master intended to sell him back into slavery in the West Indies. Sharp, a gifted civil servant and man of unquestioned genius, was determined to plead Somerset's cause. Again and again he applied to the Lord Chief Justice, Lord Mansfield, to clarify the law on the rights of ex-slaves found on British soil. At last in 1772 Mansfield was forced to concede a landmark ruling that according to English law, as it presently stood, no slave once in England could be sold back to the Colonies. This jurisdiction had major implications for

the rights of an estimated 14,000 slaves resident in British households, with most claiming their freedom in consequence.

However, Lord Mansfield cared little for the slaves. Nine years later Granville Sharp brought forward another case which angered and grieved him even more: a heinous act perpetrated by a certain Luke Collingwood, captain of the *Zong*, a slave ship. When the ship lost its way mid-Atlantic, with disease claiming the lives

Granville Sharp meets escaped slave James Somerset

of crew members and many slaves, Collingwood made a fearful decision. He would throw a large proportion of his slave cargo into the sea to enable the ship owner to claim their value on his insurance. One hundred and thirty-three healthy slaves, some shackled to prevent them struggling, were cast to the sharks; only one survived by managing to scramble back on board and then to hide. When the crime eventually came to Granville Sharp's attention, he raised it with Lord Mansfield, who refused to convict Collingwood of murder and asserted that the owners of slaves had a legal right to drown their slaves if they wished. It would have been no different, he stated, had horses been thrown overboard instead. This tragedy, and Mansfield's subsequent ruling, shocked the nation and became a rallying point in the campaign now gathering strength.

A number of other factors were also combining to create a growing national awareness of the corrupt conditions and cruelty of the slave trade. The immense cultural influence of the Enlightenment had opened the eyes of many to the dignity and basic rights of the individual, bringing about a new culture of concern for the exploited and needy. But most especially, this general humanitarian trend was fed by the powerful influences of the Evangelical Revival which had begun in the 1730s, refining the thinking of whole communities.

When John Wesley (1703–1791) himself weighed into the anti-slavery debate in 1774 by publishing his *Thoughts on Slavery*, a tract in letter form addressed to slave owners, the consciences of many newly-converted men and women were awakened to the horrors perpetrated in their name.

With convicting rhetoric Wesley traced the history and practices of slavery, and the slave trade in particular, ending with scorching and penetrating questions fired at those who prospered on such atrocities:

> *Are you a man? Then you should have a human heart. But have you indeed? What is your heart made of? Is there no such principle as compassion there? Do you never feel another's pain? Have you no sympathy, no sense of human woe, no pity for the miserable? When you saw the flowing eyes, the heaving breasts, or the bleeding sides and tortured limbs of your fellow-creatures, were you a stone, or a brute? Did you look upon them with the eyes of a tiger? When you squeezed the agonizing creatures down in the ship, or when you threw their poor mangled remains into the sea, had you no relenting? Did not one tear drop from your eye? ... Do you feel no relenting now? If you do not, you must go on, till the measure of your iniquities is full. Then will the great God deal with you as you have dealt with them and require all their blood at your hands.*

Such a tract added invaluable aid to the efforts of those seeking to awaken the public conscience of their generation, and was seed sown in fertile ground among the newly emerging evangelical Christian churches, the fruit of the revival.

Yet another account must also have fascinated Zachary Macaulay, this time of the tireless endeavours of Thomas Clarkson (1760–1846). As a twenty-six-year-old student, Clarkson was riding from Cambridge to London, carrying in his saddle-bag an essay which he had just read before the University Senate House, entitled *Is it right to make slaves of others against their will?* Clarkson had submitted this essay, written in Latin, as an entry for a competition, the title being one suggested by the Vice-Chancellor. And Clarkson had won the competition.

Night and day the tall red-haired academic had researched his material. But it had cost him dear. As he

Thomas Clarkson

learnt from many sources of the history of slavery, and in particular of the fearful sufferings of the African peoples, he had been appalled and distressed. It preyed ceaselessly on his conscience. Later he had written:

> It was but one gloomy subject from morning to night. In the daytime I was uneasy. In the night I had little rest. I sometimes never closed my eyelids for grief. It became now not so much a trial for academical reputation, as for the production of a work which might be useful to injured Africa.

On his way to London his mind was not on the accolades he had received for his prize-winning essay, but on the iniquitous practice of one race treating another as if it were sub-human, more like animals than people. As he thought of the degradation to which English merchants subjected their slaves — men, women and children dragged from their homes — he scarcely knew how to continue his journey. Words which he had written in his essay rang constantly in his ears:

They were beaten, starved, tortured, murdered at discretion: they were dead in a civil sense; they had neither name nor tribe; were incapable of a judicial process; were in short without appeal. Poor unfortunate men! to be deprived of all possible protection! to suffer the bitterest of injuries without the possibility of redress! to be condemned unheard! to be murdered with impunity! to be considered as dead in that state, the very members of which they were supporting by their labours!

Overcome by his thoughts, Clarkson dismounted from time to time and walked. He tells us what happened next:

I frequently tried to persuade myself in these intervals that the contents of my Essay could not be true. The more, however, I reflected upon them ... the more I gave them credit. Coming within sight of Wades Mill in Hertfordshire I sat down disconsolate on the turf by the roadside and held my horse. Here a thought came into my mind, that if the contents of the Essay were true, it was time some person should see these calamities to an end.

And who could that person be? Surely he himself must bear the responsibility. From that moment on Thomas Clarkson, who had been preparing to enter the Church of England ministry, dedicated his life to one great end: to abolish the slave trade and if possible slavery itself. As he remounted his horse, Clarkson was now a determined man, a man with a mission. First he stayed with friends who were also concerned about the slave trade; next he decided to translate his essay from the Latin and distribute it countrywide, raising both knowledge of the slave trade and indignation against it.

So when Thomas Clarkson met Granville Sharp he found a man of kindred spirit. Together they joined with ten others, many of them Quakers, who had already formed a Committee for the Abolition of the Slave Trade, and dedicated themselves to the eradication of such evils. Assuming the new and bolder title of the Society for Effecting the Abolition of the Slave Trade, they all knew they were up against enormous opposition. According to William Pitt (1759–1806), who had become prime minister in 1783, profits secured by the slave labour in the West Indies accounted for 80% of the country's overseas income. How would Parliament ever agree to the abolition of so lucrative a source of the nation's wealth? Nevertheless, fortified by their new members, the Society resolved to do all in its power to change the mindset of a country which undoubtedly viewed slavery as indispensable.

Thomas Clarkson became its travelling agent: his commission was to amass as many facts as possible about the slave trade in order to feed and fire effective parliamentary representation against it. As he travelled he was appalled by what he learnt. In Bristol, one of the main ports used by the slave ships, he was scarcely able to believe the stories of horror and cruelty reported to him. Even the crews on the ships were handled with barbarity, many of the men dying from the harsh treatment they received. More than ready to share their stories with Clarkson, survivors furnished him with fearful details of the conditions on board the ships. 'I was agonised to think that this trade could last another day. I was in a state of agitation from morning to night,' he recollected. He managed to gather a collection of instruments of torture: thumbscrews, shackles and even gadgets used to force open the mouths of slaves refusing to eat. These he carried with him, demonstrating their use to the horrified citizens he addressed in public lectures.

In 1788 Clarkson was continually on the road, at one period travelling as much as 1600 miles on horseback in two months. During a visit to Plymouth he met a former slave-ship surgeon, Alexander Falconbridge, who was prepared to give him detailed first-hand information of the fearful overcrowding on the ships. From his information, Clarkson learnt that as many as 482 slaves could be crammed into the hold of a ship. Packed side by side, often shackled in pairs, these desperate people were forced to lie in their own and others' excrement and vomit, sores breaking out on their bodies as their limbs rubbed incessantly on the wooden floor.

Clarkson translated these figures into diagram form, using the measurements of a ship called the *Brookes*, docked in the Thames at that time. The result was horrifying. Seeing the potential of this appalling image, the Society for Effecting the Abolition of the Slave Trade had some 8,000 printed and distributed — a picture that would become famous as an illustration of the abuse it was fighting to abolish.

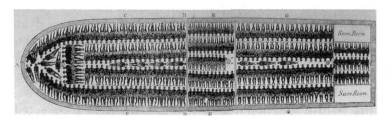

Plan of lower deck with stowage of 292 slaves,
some under shelves with only 2ft 7ins of height between.

Clarkson rode throughout England, Scotland and Wales distributing leaflets, making speeches, forming abolitionist committees and gathering data on the conditions of the slave trade to present before Parliament. During the many nights spent in local taverns along the way, Clarkson encouraged open discussion of the issues at stake. Sometimes mugged, often in danger of his life, always weary and sickened at heart, he persevered. His contribution to the anti-slave trade movement was inestimable.

Meanwhile Granville Sharp was wrestling with another intractable problem. As a result of his own intervention with Lord Mansfield and the ruling he had forced through in 1772, thousands of freed slaves were wandering the streets of London. They were often without employment and frequently destitute. It had become imperative to make some provision for them. Why not send them back to West Africa to settle on land purchased from one of the chieftains in the area? This would help solve the problem and provide proof that Africans could manage their own affairs and succeed.

In April 1787 the first ship-load of settlers set sail. A motley selection of individuals, it consisted of four hundred ex-slaves, a number of white men with criminal records and about sixty prostitutes. Destined for an area known as Sierra Leone, a fertile tract of land of about twenty square miles, it looked a hopeful project. But the new settlers were scarcely fit for the challenge and ill-prepared for the conditions they were to meet. Incessant spring rains meant they could not cultivate the land, drunkenness was rife, malaria and other tropical diseases wrought havoc. Some absconded and others died of starvation. Then came a devastating blow. In

1789, only two years after the first ship had sailed, a local African chieftain, angry over some offence, set fire to the new settlement, appropriately called Granville Town. Now the project seemed doomed.

The destruction of the small town was a serious setback for the Society. Considerable finance would be needed to retrieve the situation, and no one proved more willing and able to help than the young banker and Member of Parliament for Southwark, Henry Thornton (1760–1815). A brilliant financier, Henry learnt early in his life, from his father's example, of the privilege of generosity and like him insisted that all income above his immediate bachelor needs was to be donated to Christian causes. Although his name now appears in the records for his far-sighted financial policies in a time of monetary turmoil, the noblest and most lasting contribution of his life was the support he gave to men like Thomas Clarkson, Granville Sharp and others whose goal was to right the social evils of the day.

One of the first major undertakings financed by Thornton was the rescue of Granville Sharp's failed project in Sierra Leone. A new company was soon formed, the Sierra Leone Company, with the board consisting of Granville Sharp as president, Henry Thornton as both chairman and one of the directors, Thomas Clarkson, Thomas Babington and, most significantly, William Wilberforce (1759–1833). Wilberforce, a friend of Babington's from student days at Cambridge and now MP for Yorkshire, was born in Hull in 1759, and had represented that city since the age of twenty-one. Cheerful, rich and sociable, the young man had little time for God until 1784, when he went on a leisurely tour of France with his old school-teacher, Isaac Milner. A brilliant mathematician, but more importantly an earnest Christian, Milner spent hours talking to Wilberforce as they travelled. These long conversations, coupled with a reading of Philip Doddridge's *The Rise and Progress of Religion on the Soul,* led to Wilberforce's conversion and a dramatic turnabout in his lifestyle and priorities. With further encouragement from John Thornton and also from John Newton, vicar of St Mary Woolnoth, the young politician now saw that he could serve God by using his parliamentary position to sponsor moral changes in the nation.

Thomas Clarkson and his friends soon learnt of the great change in Wilberforce and of the new motivation governing all his hopes and ambitions for the welfare of his fellow men. Who better, wondered Clarkson, to enlist in the fight against the slave trade? Tentatively he booked an appointment to see the young politician at his home in Old Palace Yard, Westminster, early in 1787. In his hand Clarkson carried a copy of his essay translated from the Latin. Yet surprisingly he found himself unaccountably diffident in Wilberforce's presence. Hesitating to press the issue at this first interview, he merely hinted at the fearful abuses of the African slave trade and left his essay in Wilberforce's hand. The only assurance he received from Wilberforce, who had in fact already given the issue much thought, was that the cause was 'near his heart' and he would like to spend more time learning about it.

The essay certainly gave Wilberforce any extra information he may have needed. In March of that same year, 1787, Clarkson invited him to a dinner function together with a number of other prominent men. His response now to the subject of the slave trade was altogether more positive. By

October 1787 he was totally committed and in 1789, the very year that Zachary Macaulay returned from Jamaica, Wilberforce delivered the first of his many speeches in the Commons on the issue — one that lasted three and a half hours, and demonstrated the iniquity of present practices of maltreating our fellow human beings, especially in the light of the coming judgement of God.

Perhaps Zachary read an astonishing autobiography also published that year — *The Interesting Narrative of the Life*

Olaudah Aquiano

of Olaudah Equiano, the African, written by himself. Heartrending in its details, it described the capture of a small African boy and his sister by black slave traders, their arduous march to the coast, their sale to a European merchant and their subsequent life in Virginia. The book was an instant bestseller. Here was an authentic account by a former slave recounting both his own and his people's sufferings.[1] This publication proved yet another potent factor in awakening the conscience of the people to crimes perpetuated in their name.

In January 1790, Wilberforce lobbied the Treasury to allow the newly founded Sierra Leone Company to purchase a small ship called the *Lapwing* presently moored in the Government dockyards and awaiting demolition. For the trifling sum of £180, the *Lapwing* passed into the ownership of the company. Newly equipped, it proved a fine vessel and was immediately requisitioned to sail to Sierra Leone under the command of John Clarkson (1764–1828), Thomas Clarkson's younger brother. With him sailed Alexander Falconbridge, the former ship surgeon who had assisted Thomas with details of the overcrowding on the slave ships. Falconbridge's commission was to ascertain the state of the colony, gather the scattered remnant of settlers and reorganize the life of the settlement. Finding some sixty-four of the original settlers, Falconbridge brought them together and, in conjunction with John Clarkson as temporary governor of the colony, began the rebuilding of burnt-out Granville Town, changing its name to Freetown.

With a more secure refuge for freed slaves on the west coast of Africa, the great task of abolishing the trade itself had begun in earnest and hopes ran high that the vision and goal might soon be accomplished. Men of the calibre of Granville Sharp, Henry Thornton, Thomas Clarkson, Thomas Babington and William Wilberforce himself were united in one common endeavour. And listening in to their conversations, now one with them in spiritual life and purpose, was a sharp-minded and gifted young man — Zachary Macaulay.

Note

1. Questions have been raised as to the authenticity of Aquiano's claim to have been born in a remote Nigerian village and sold as a slave. But the power and effect of his publication remains undisputed. The disclosure of the atrocity on board the *Zong* came from Aquiano.

4

ON PROBATION AND BEYOND

As Thomas Babington considered the obvious potential in his young brother-in-law, the plan that had been steadily taking shape in his mind became a fixed purpose. Hidden beneath Zachary's overbearing ways and domineering manner Babington recognized a man of extraordinary talent and untapped abilities. There could surely be a role for him in the great project constantly under discussion among the visitors to Rothley Temple — the rebuilding and development of the haven for ex-slaves in West Africa. Tentatively at first, Babington suggested to his friends that it might be worth sending Zachary out to Sierra Leone for a trial period as an 'observer' to test his wisdom and aptitude in handling complex and unpredictable problems in a volatile situation.

The proposal was greeted warmly by Henry Thornton, Granville Sharp and the other directors of the nascent Sierra Leone Company. With life and motivations transformed by the gospel, Zachary Macaulay, now almost twenty-three, accepted the suggestion eagerly. As he had listened to the many conversations between Thomas Babington and his friends, he had found his thoughts dwelling constantly on the issues they were discussing — Sierra Leone and the campaign to abolish the slave trade altogether. Perhaps, with his training in banking and his experiences in Jamaica, he might be of some service in that cause and possibly make amends for the past in some measure.

As a result, early in 1791 Zachary left British shores once more, this time bound for Sierra Leone. With him went a Church of England clergyman, Nathaniel Gilbert, whom the directors had commissioned to take spiritual charge of the infant colony. The friendship of a wise and older Christian during the voyage and later in Sierra Leone itself was both helpful and encouraging for the younger man. 'He is a man of real piety, of a meek and gentle spirit,' reported Zachary as he wrote to Thomas Babington when he reached West Africa. Zachary was on probation, although he may not have realized it.

The humid climate, relieved only by the hot dry winds from the desert, the constant raainfall through many months of the year, debilitating fevers, constant bickering and plotting among the settlers — Zachary met all with an unruffled spirit. Where decisions rested on his judgement, he showed himself calm and balanced. Meanwhile he continued to follow with deep interest the labours of the men who had become his friends as they struggled against the odds to convince Parliament's sceptical and prejudiced politicians to ban the slave trade. Sitting in his bleak and often leaking wooden hut, Macaulay would have read Wilberforce's

impassioned words to the House of Commons in April
1791:

> Let us not despair; it is a blessed cause, and success, ere
> long, will crown our exertions. Already we have gained one
> victory; we have obtained, for these poor creatures, the
> recognition of their human nature, which, for a while was
> most shamefully denied. This is the first fruits of our efforts;
> let us persevere and our triumph will be complete. Never,
> never will we desist till we have wiped away this scandal
> from the Christian name, released ourselves from the load
> of guilt, under which we at present labour, and extinguished
> every trace of this bloody traffic, of which our posterity,
> looking back to the history of these enlightened times, will
> scarce believe that it has been suffered to exist so long a
> disgrace and dishonour to this country.

When Zachary returned to England early in 1792 he
discovered he had gained the unanimous appreciation of all
the directors of the Sierra Leone Company for his conduct,
resolution and reliability during the months he had been
away. Before long the board approached the young man,
now twenty-four, asking him undertake the responsible task
of becoming assistant governor of the colony. Here was a
service that God had been preparing for Zachary throughout
his varied and unusual life experiences, grievous in many
ways and yet clearly under the overarching purposes of God.

During the rest of 1792 Zachary remained in London,
helping Henry Thornton in the many plans and projects
for Sierra Leone which his new appointment would entail.
These months forged a deep friendship and confidence

between the two men, one that formed the bedrock of all Zachary's future labours and decisions. From Thornton he gained a clear understanding of the responsibilities that he must shoulder as Assistant Governor.

Towards the end of 1792 Zachary turned yet again from the comforts of life in England to face the uncertainties and privations of life in Sierra Leone. This time he was to serve under the guidance of William Dawes (1762–1836), chosen to be Governor in place of John Clarkson, whose appointment had been only temporary. Zachary had nothing but praise for Dawes; his wisdom and discretion won his respect. Writing of him later, Zachary paid tribute to his 'great sweetness of disposition and most unbending principles', adding that in all the period that they worked together not an unkind word or look passed between them — a noble testimony considering the climate, the shared accommodation and the constant perplexities that arose in the management of the colony.

Zachary soon discovered that considerable changes had taken place in his absence from Sierra Leone during most of 1792. Most noticeable was the large influx of new settlers, slaves recently liberated following the American War of Independence. Fearful of defeat in a war fought between 1775 and 1783, the British government had granted pledges of freedom to any slaves who would enlist to fight on the British side. When Britain finally conceded defeat and granted the colonies their independence, a home had to be found for more than 3000 freed slaves. The new American government decided to send them to Nova Scotia with promises of grants of land for cultivation. It sounded good, but when the ex-slaves arrived, they found themselves confined to a desolate, frequently cold and windswept peninsula. To make things worse, the agricultural land promised was either withheld or proved barren and almost impossible to cultivate. Many were brought to destitution, some to near starvation.

Learning of the situation, the elderly Selina, Countess of Huntingdon (1707–1791), financed the services of a black pastor, John Marrant, to live and work among them. Converted under George Whitefield in Carolina, Marrant was an ideal appointment and was able to establish a number of churches in Nova Scotia. Then in 1792 news filtered through of a haven set up for freed slaves in Sierra Leone. Enthusiastically, a large proportion of the black community, many of them members of these 'Countess of Huntingdon' churches, petitioned to be transferred to West Africa.[1] All their expenses were met by the British government and each was promised a certain acreage of land according to the size of his family. John Clarkson, still temporary governor at the time, had travelled to Nova Scotia as an escort on the hazardous crossing. Sadly many, already weakened by their hardships in Nova Scotia, died during the voyage, with only 1131 out of a probable 2000 surviving. By the time Zachary Macaulay and William Dawes arrived in Sierra Leone in January 1793 the newcomers had begun to settle, and actually formed the bulk of the colony's population, a fact that changed the aspect and future of Sierra Leone.

Dawes and Macaulay were far from being the only ones appointed and financed by the Sierra Leone Company to serve in the colony. Medical staff, school teachers, men to liaise with slave traders, plantation overseers, legal advisors: one hundred and nineteen men and women in all had been sent to Sierra Leone since early in 1791 with the hope of affording the colony its best hope of success as a viable refuge for freed slaves. But tragically by the end of 1792 almost half of these dedicated workers had died. The extremes of climate coupled with the intensity of tropical fevers such as malaria, dengue fever and typhoid fever had been mowing down staff members at a frightening rate. Of the sixty that remained when Macaulay arrived, a further twenty returned to England and by the end of 1793 only about forty were left, many of them struggling with illness. This resulted in a heavy burden of work for Zachary and Governor Dawes and called for enormous stamina, especially for Zachary, who had already suffered from serious bouts of malaria.

One of his first and least enviable tasks was that of establishing cordial relationships with the managers of the slave depots. Some of these depots were situated on off-shore islands, while others had been set up in tributaries along the mighty Sierra Leone River which ran inland for twenty-five miles. Of these, Bunce (or 'Bance') Island and Gambia Island were the nearest to Freetown, with Bunce under the control of a Liverpool merchant company and Gambia in the possession of the French. The resident managers of these slave depots, men of doubtful morals and unsavoury character, were responsible for arranging the sale of slaves in exchange for goods commissioned by the African chieftains. Any dealings with them were problematic at best. Zachary also had to negotiate with the managers of a number of more distant slave depots, including Sherbro Island, eighty miles south of Freetown, and the Isles of Los to the north. Considering

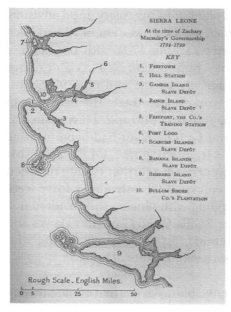

SIERRA LEONE
At the time of Zachary
Macaulay's Governorship
1794–1799

KEY

1. Freetown
2. Hill Station
3. Gambia Island
    Slave Depôt
4. Bance Island
    Slave Depôt
5. Freeport, the Co.'s
    Trading Station
6. Port Logo
7. Scarcies Islands
    Slave Depôt
8. Banana Islands
    Slave Depôt
9. Sherbro Island
    Slave Depôt
10. Bullom Shore
    Co.'s Plantation

Rough Scale – English Miles.
0   5   25   50

that Freetown and the Sierra Leone Company itself represented a direct challenge to the business interests of these men, it speaks highly for Zachary's ability that he managed any degree of civil rapport with them at all. On occasions he found himself having to placate them when their slaves managed to escape and sought refuge in Freetown; at other times he had to confront them over instances of unprovoked cruelty.

Sometimes the directors back in England were unhappy with Zachary's decisions. To them he seemed to be compromising basic principles when he sent runaway slaves seeking refuge in Freetown back to their masters. Surely he was undermining the whole purpose of the colony. Such misunderstandings arose because the men in England could not appreciate the delicate balance between Sierra Leone and its neighbours; how easily bare tolerance could flare into antagonism; nor did they realize how dependent the colony was at times on these unscrupulous men, even for its continued existence and the provision of essential supplies. If Zachary had not cultivated these good relationships, the probability of Sierra Leone surviving as a colony was slim.

Zachary was to be responsible for the smooth day-to-day management of the colony and especially the handling of problems relating to the settlers, both the handful of originals and the recent arrivals, many of whom would prove recalcitrant and uncooperative. Dawes, on the other hand, had charge of overall policies and decisions. With a depleted staff only limited progress could be made in developing the agriculture of the colony or in setting up trade outlets with the surrounding tribal areas. But despite the problems, 1793 was a fruitful year in many ways, with an elaborate system of justice put in place bearing all the hallmarks of Zachary's legal turn of mind. Families were each divided into groups of ten, with every group appointing a 'tithingman' to oversee its affairs. For each ten 'tithingmen', one known as a 'hundreder' was appointed to be responsible for all matters that could not be settled lower down the chain. And for intractable problems and crimes a jury system was established, with serious offenders sent back to England to stand trial. In addition to this well-thought-out system of justice, Zachary and William Dawes also managed to oversee the beginnings of a thriving school for the settlers' children and for illiterate adults. Zachary reports in December 1793:

> Our schools are a cheering sight; three hundred children fill them and most of the grown persons who cannot read crowd to the evening schools. We have made a schoolmaster of almost every black man in the colony who reads or writes well enough. The business of instruction proceeds so rapidly within the colony that in the course of a year or two there will be few who will not be able to read their Bibles.

Zachary had one further duty each day. Despite rain, heat and fever, he sat down at his make-shift desk and wrote a long and graphic report of day-to-day events in the colony for Henry Thornton and the directors back in England, men who were eagerly awaiting his accounts of progress and problems. With his already impaired sight, such laborious and detailed records demonstrate his total and dedicated commitment to the task.

But just when all seemed to be progressing as satisfactorily as possible, a further crisis arose. William Dawes, Macaulay's friend, mentor and senior colleague, was taken seriously ill. The only hope of a cure seemed to lie in his immediate return to England. Knowing that unless Dawes made a remarkable and complete recovery, the colony would lose its governor, the board of directors appointed Zachary Macaulay as his successor.

And in March 1794, little more than a year after Zachary had first taken up the position of Assistant Governor, he stood on the quayside watching the ship *Harpy* sailing into the distance, carrying William Dawes back to England. Not quite twenty-six years old, Zachary knew that the burden for this vital project of creating a haven for freed slaves in Sierra Leone was now falling solely on his shoulders. In three short years he had progressed from probation to a position of ultimate responsibility for Sierra Leone.

Note

1. Many of these settlers carried with them their Countess of Huntingdon Hymnbooks and established a number of churches that still survive today as part of the Countess of Huntingdon Connexion.

5

DISASTER STRIKES

No sooner had the *Harpy* disappeared from view than some of the settlers took the opportunity to riot. Simmering discontent, largely on the part of those from Nova Scotia, broke out into open violence. Aggrieved that they were being denied their perceived rights, the newcomers had also struggled with the strictures imposed on them by communal life in the colony. They were not prepared to engage in the vital work of agriculture, which they considered degrading in their status as freed men and women. And now all their pent-up feelings welled over. Macaulay's newly-erected company office was plundered and papers, including his private journal, scattered and destroyed. For some days the situation looked ugly. But with a combination of clear-headed composure and steely determination, Zachary managed to quell the uprising, arresting the ringleaders. With these shipped off to England to stand trial, he himself felt sufficiently in control of affairs to grant a general pardon to all others who had taken part. 'What I bless God for above all', he later wrote, 'is the collectedness of mind he has given me throughout the whole business; he made my way so clear I scarcely felt any embarrassment.'

While Macaulay's own task looked daunting enough, the prospect of abolishing the slave trade altogether now seemed more remote than ever. Gone were the buoyant hopes which had sustained the abolitionists in England at the outset of the parliamentary campaign. And the cause? Fear: fear in the wake of the French Revolution which had erupted into violence following the storming of the Bastille and the revolt of the peasant population in 1789. What would happen, Parliament argued, if the people of England rose up in the same way, overturned the social order and started beheading the ruling elite without mercy?

This was not all. During August 1791, in the French-held colony of San Domingo, now Haiti, 100,000 slaves revolted against their white overlords, repaying years of oppression with murder, rape, torture and unrestrained destruction of property, all mixed in with wild voodoo religious ceremonies. English slave owners listened with horror to reports that up to four thousand whites had been killed or injured. What would happen if their own slave population in the Caribbean followed such an example? Even William Pitt, prime minister and friend of William Wilberforce, whose support for the abolition of the slave trade had been so vital to their aspirations, suddenly stalled on the issue. An almost mindless fear, coupled with a self-centred determination to protect their own interests, replaced all humanitarian thinking. Hope of gaining a parliamentary majority for the cause faded. The eighty-seven-year-old John Wesley, writing in February 1791, less than a week before his death, had

words of consolation and
encouragement for William
Wilberforce: 'Unless God
had raised you up for this
very thing, you will be worn
out by the opposition of men
and devils, but if God be for
you who can be against you.
Go in the name of God and
in the power of his might...'

John Wesley in later years

Although Parliament even-
tually passed a bill in April
1792 for the 'gradual' aboli-
tion of the slave trade, such a resolution was meaningless,
as Wilberforce and his friends knew well. The word 'gradual', introduced by Henry Dundas, the Home Secretary, was
really a subtle form of saying 'never'; and in any case the
House of Lords could only promise to set up an inquiry into
the issues.

Meanwhile, events in revolutionary France continued at a
frightening speed. Louis XVI and Queen Marie Antoinette
were arrested, imprisoned and in January 1793 were
brutally guillotined, followed by more than 20,000 other
citizens who had held a position in society. The new French
government soon grabbed the opportunity of the general
upheaval to initiate a series of wars, known as the French
Revolutionary Wars, which aimed at establishing French
dominance in Holland, Germany and further afield. An
excitable, undisciplined army called the sans-culottes was
recruited to serve the purpose, made up of raw peasantry

from the French countryside, willing to commit atrocities in pursuit of personal gain.

Surely, trouble from such a source could not reach as far as Sierra Leone, thought Zachary Macaulay. Nor did he suspect anything when seven ships, all flying the English flag, sailed into the mouth of the Sierra Leone River as he was conducting evening worship on 28 September 1794. Everyone had assumed that these vessels were bringing supplies of food and other necessities to the colony. Then the distant sound of gunfire puzzled and alarmed the gathered worshippers. Not until first light the next day did the startling truth become clear. These were not English ships at all, but French warships in disguise, each fully armed.

The French were intent on destruction; this much was clear to Zachary and his staff as they debated desperately what to do. They must save as much of the colony's property as they could. But would resistance of any sort be possible? Soon they knew the answer as gunshot whistled overhead. When the veranda of the government building where they were sitting was peppered with bullets, they knew no alternative remained but an abject surrender. As the firing continued into the town itself, some were killed, others seriously injured.

Unruly sans-culotte troops began streaming ashore, guided by an American slave trader who had long nursed a grudge against the colony because some of his slaves had sought protection there. They presented a strange sight. Some were dressed in women's clothing, others arrayed in multiple outfits, the spoils of earlier forays. Everywhere they went, they burnt, looted and defaced the properties.

Desperate to restrict the damage, Zachary hastily made his way to the Commodore's cabin on board the flagship of the French fleet. Perhaps he would be able at least to control his men and stop the destruction. But as he climbed the gangplank and stepped on deck, Zachary was horrified at the appalling conditions he discovered. 'The quarter-deck was crowded by a set of ragamuffins whose appearance beggared every previous description ... the stench and filth exceeded anything I had ever witnessed in any ship.'

The Commodore received Macaulay civilly enough, but informed him that Freetown's great offence in the eyes of the French was its English governors. He would try, so he said, to protect the homes of the African settlers from being burnt down, but could hold out little hope for the government buildings. As Zachary returned to Freetown some hours later a scene of utter devastation met his eyes. His own headquarters had already been ransacked:

> The sight of my own and the accountant's offices almost sickened me. Every desk, every shelf, together with the printing and copying presses, had been completely demolished in the search for money. The floors were strewn with types, papers, and leaves of books, and I had the mortification to see a great part of my own labour and of the labour of others for several years totally destroyed. At the other end of the house I found telescopes ... barometers, thermometers and electrical machines lying about in fragments. The view of the town library filled me with concern. The volumes were tossed about and defaced with the utmost wantonness, and if they happened to bear any resemblance to Bibles they were torn in pieces and trampled upon.

Everywhere Zachary looked he saw wild French soldiers hacking up and trashing anything that was not of immediate use to them. Pigs bred for meat for the colony were being shot indiscriminately — hundreds already lay dead — others, squealing in terror, were rushing madly around the streets adding to the confusion. In his own quarters more than a hundred and fifty chickens had been strangled. Unkempt-looking fellows now occupied the main rooms of his house and even had the audacity to invite Macaulay to share a rudimentary meal of stewed chicken and boiled pork.

In such desperate circumstances, Macaulay records the unexpected composure that he and members of the staff experienced:

> We found we had lost very little by the change. We were free from pain; we felt neither cold, nor hunger nor thirst; in short we found out that happiness does not consist in the number of things we possess... Our prospects as to lodging, clothing and food were very gloomy, but ... we were not tortured with doubt or suspense.

However, this surreal calm was shattered when night fell. Having drunk themselves into senseless hilarity, the French soldiers 'entertained' Zachary all night long with accounts of atrocities they planned to commit. Most notably they elaborated on schemes of revenge they determined to vent on the English prime minister, William Pitt, when they got him in their power.

The Commodore of the fleet, who appeared sorry about the situation but quite helpless to stop it or control the wanton

damage wreaked on the colony, invited Macaulay to sleep
in his cabin. A little quieter it certainly was, but even so,
sleep was scarcely possible. Apart from the stench and filth
everywhere, Zachary had no bedding, for it had all been
stolen, and not even a sheet did the Commodore offer as a
covering despite the cold of the nights. And still the random
shooting went on. Not satisfied with the level of ruin wreaked
so far, the ignorant peasant troops destroyed anything that
reminded them of civilized living: lamps, mirrors, tableware,
books, furniture — nothing escaped.

Even more distressing for Zachary Macaulay and the other
members of the Freetown team were the fickle actions of
some of the settlers themselves — the very people they were
there to help. Instead of trying to salvage anything belonging
to the Governor and his associates, they hid away in the
surrounding forests during the day, returning at night under
cover of darkness to join the looters, grabbing any item of
value they could find and then sneaking back into the forest
with their ill-gotten spoils.

All government property was torched. Nothing escaped
the conflagration. Even the ships belonging to Freetown
lying at anchor in the river were set alight. Having lost so
much Zachary could only view the ruin of all that he had
built up over the last few years with a numb indifference: He
describes the scene:

> I entered the church. The pulpit was broken in pieces, the
> prayer books and Bibles torn and defaced; the clock disfig-
> ured and rendered useless. The Commodore had promised
> to save the church but I did not believe him. The chemist's

shop was a heap of confusion, every bottle, every jar was
broken, and the medicines were totally destroyed.

In all this calamity, Zachary, his staff and many of the settlers
who had remained faithful and trustworthy, could only join
in casting themselves on the mercy and compassion of God.
Zachary freely admitted that in so desperate a situation, with
food running short and medicines for the sick and injured
all but destroyed, his faith was tested to the limit.

On 9 October, almost two weeks after the invasion had
begun, Zachary heard that a packet of letters from England
addressed to him had been salvaged from one of the ships and
placed in the charge of the Commodore. Macaulay hurried
aboard the captain's ship eager to claim his correspondence.
What followed was perhaps one of the darkest moments
emotionally of the whole sorry episode for Zachary himself.
The Commodore merely replied coolly that he was just
too late. A few minutes before he had thrown them all
overboard. In dismay Zachary looked over the side of the
ship and saw his vital correspondence floating about in the
water. He begged the use of a small boat to gather up as
much as he could. But the Commodore, whose sympathies
were only skin deep, refused. 'I strove with him. I entreated.
I protested. It was all in vain. He remained inflexible.' This
last blow, though seemingly small in comparison to all that
had already taken place, was almost too much for the brave
Governor to endure. He continues:

Nothing had yet happened materially to disturb my mind,
but this stroke affected me very forcibly. My regret for the
loss of the letters, and my indignation at such unworthy

treatment, such wanton cruelty, unhinged me not a little...
We came ashore dispirited and mortified and disappointed
beyond measure.

Food was now running short. Wheat, rice, sugar and rum
— a staple drink — were all in scarce supply. Medicines
were almost unobtainable after the wholesale destruction
of all the colony's reserves, particularly of quinine, so vital
for combating malaria. Stocks of gunpowder and all means
of self-defence were almost exhausted. Had it not been for
the good relationships that Zachary Macaulay had forged
with the slave traders, the settlers of Freetown and its staff
might well have perished. With money hidden from the
marauding hands of the sans-culottes, Zachary was able to
purchase basic necessities from the slave traders. Even the
untrustworthy Commodore felt some pangs of pity for what
had happened and sent a few provisions ashore.

But if the Freetown settlers were short of food, so too were
the French invaders. And on 12 October, just two weeks
after the first gunshots had shattered the peace of a Sunday
morning, those seven French ships with their deceptive
English flags sailed off down the coast of Africa, doubtless
looking for more targets for their plundering agenda. Before
they left, the Commodore gave Freetown a further problem
to handle. One hundred and twenty English seamen,
captured during earlier encounters were being held in the
hold of one of the ships. Most were ill through malnutrition
and filthy conditions, some were dying. These the French
decided to abandon in Sierra Leone in the care of Zachary
Macaulay and his settlers — an added burden in an already
desperate situation. Zachary estimated the destruction the

French had inflicted on the entire area at more than £400,000 in eighteenth-century values.

In this critical situation of loss, sickness and fear, Macaulay's sterling qualities of stoical endurance and courage, qualities that had kept him alive during the worst periods of his days in Jamaica, shone out. Ill himself, desperately short of sleep and emotionally drained, he did not despair. He resolutely refused to take any of the dwindling supplies of quinine for the relief of his own fever, and instead began the demanding work of restoring some semblance of order in the chaotic aftermath of the invasion.

Within a week rebuilding work had begun. Another storeroom to house provisions was needed and immediately above it a new church was to be built, eighty feet in length by twenty in width. Most important was his tactful dealings with the settlers who had joined the looters and had company property stashed away in the forest. Sternly insisting that all stolen property must be returned, he yet showed genuine compassion with his demands. Unfounded rumours had been circulating among the settlers — clearly an attempt to justify their own behaviour — and each day it was a different tale: Macaulay had betrayed them to the French; he had allowed their homes to be robbed; and many other more scurrilous allegations. Thanks to Macaulay, most settlers quietly restored stolen property without having to admit to theft in the first place, thus saving damaging recriminations.

The sick sailors deposited by the French presented a further problem. Three or four were dying each day, and in spite of allowing them the best share of available rations and medicines, Zachary could only report that 'the prospect is truly melancholy'. Still fighting fever himself, the intrepid governor pressed ahead with his rebuilding programme, and within three weeks was able to report in his regular journal for the Sierra Leone directors in England that the new church was almost ready for use.

But the physical cost was high. At last Macaulay succumbed to the malaria he had been battling and by the beginning of November was forced to take to his bed. 'Almost all of us were now laid up,' he reported. Even the doctors on the staff were sick. As news of the devastation and then of Zachary's own serious condition reached England, Henry Thornton and his friends knew they must act quickly. William Dawes, the previous governor, now much improved in health, was immediately despatched to West Africa to take over from Macaulay. Zachary must come home on the next ship available, Thornton insisted.

Knowing that he had laid the foundations for a recovery from the blow that had struck the infant Sierra Leone project, Zachary was grateful for an opportunity to return to England and regain his strength once more. He could argue with confidence that despite the huge financial loss the Sierra Leone Company had sustained, Freetown could be rebuilt and become successful once more. And so Zachary departed — but as we shall see, not by the orthodox route you would expect of a sick man.

Note

1. Without knee breeches.

6

FRIENDS — OLD AND NEW

The *Anna* was waiting in dock at the mouth of the Sierra Leone River; meanwhile, her captain was busy collecting his assignment of slaves to be sold in far-off Barbados. Slowly the desperate struggling men and women were being wrenched from their families and packed into small boats to take them across to the *Anna*. Just as the ship was ready to sail, the captain received an unexpected and unwelcome request. The governor of Sierra Leone, none other than Zachary Macaulay himself, was asking to be taken on board as a passenger to Barbados. Was he wishing to act the part of a spy? Quite unwilling to entertain such a suggestion, the captain protested that his ship was overcrowded already and he had no room at all for passengers.

A streak of steely determination in the twenty-seven-year-old Scotsman's character had served Zachary well in the past and again his persistence won the day. Grudgingly, the captain of the *Anna* conceded that he could sling a hammock for Macaulay over some of the slaves in the hold and allow his strange passenger to sleep there. The stench, he warned menacingly, would be almost unbearable until the Atlantic winds started to blow through.

It did indeed seem odd that Zachary Macaulay, an ill man, should choose to sail to Barbados in such a vessel, experiencing at first-hand the miseries of the infamous 'Middle Passage'. Surely it made much better sense to sail directly to England in the relative comfort of one of the Sierra Leone Company's own ships. But such a choice was typical of Zachary's single-minded zeal and dedication to the cause of abolishing the slave trade, one shared by all the men now known as the abolitionists. Macaulay was already well acquainted with the harshness of life in Jamaica; he had overseen the establishment of Sierra Leone, and now determined to complete his personal knowledge of the slave trade by observing first-hand the sufferings of the slaves during the Middle Passage. Only then would he be equipped to represent the horrors endured by these unfortunate men and women with conviction and accuracy.

So on 6 May 1795 Macaulay boarded the *Anna* for a voyage that would last for three weeks — a vast improvement on the three months it had once taken for such a journey. He had no need to worry about a slave insurrection, the captain assured Macaulay, for anyone likely to cause problems would be shackled in the hold, with the most troublesome ones chained not by wrists and ankles only but also by the neck.

Day after day Zachary carefully recorded all he witnessed on board the *Anna*, for these were the facts to be used as ammunition supplied to William Wilberforce and other politicians for future challenges to Parliament. It soon became evident that many of Macaulay's fellow-travellers longed only to die; one woman attempted to drown herself; others refused to eat. Under the threat of being whipped with the cat-o'-nine-tails some made a pretence of eating, but spat the food into the sea as soon as the officer on duty had turned his back. Perhaps exercise was the answer to their depression, thought the captain, as he ordered the slaves to dance up and down on the deck. Again, only out of fear of the 'cat' being administered did reluctant slaves oblige.

At last land was in sight and on 29 May the *Anna* docked in the natural harbour of Bridgetown, Barbados. Zachary mulled over his experiences: for him the trauma had now almost finished but for the slaves it was only just beginning. 'Their cup is full of pure unmingled sorrow, the bitterness of which is unalloyed by almost a single ray of hope' was his verdict on his strange voyage. But Macaulay did more than merely note the physical sufferings of the slaves. He was also making a detailed analysis of the conditions he discovered on the ship, and planning his further investigations when he arrived in Barbados. With the mind of a statistician and a flair for meticulous accuracy, Macaulay's future usefulness and the most enduring contribution of his life was beginning to take shape. Once in Barbados he intended to collect, chronicle and evaluate every circumstance relating to the treatment of slaves on the island, covering a sweeping range of topics. All this was in readiness for convincing a hardened parliamentary opposition of the absolute necessity of reform, paving the way for the total abolition of the slave trade.

Exhaustive lists have survived of the subjects Macaulay covered during his stay. A bewildering array of issues attracted his attention: the exact numbers of slaves, the ratio of men to women; the percentage increase or decrease of slave numbers in recent years. He asked many questions: was any religious instruction being given to the slaves, how prevalent was polygamy among them and was marriage encouraged? He studied the common diseases of the slave population and investigated the degree of medical care given, and especially the treatment of tetanus for injured slaves. Abortion attempts, infanticide and the prevalence of venereal disease were all on his lists of enquiry. So too were matters concerning childbirth, infant mortality, aftercare of mothers, efficiency and practices of midwives — nothing escaped his acute observation and ever-ready notebook.

In addition, Macaulay studied the equity of the judicial system, or perhaps the lack of it, particularly when any offence was committed among the slave population. What misdemeanours received the death penalty? Zachary had an amazingly retentive memory. His records were fair and exact and every enquiry thorough to the last detail. Certainly, this man, ill or well, and with partial eyesight never wasted a moment. With his notebooks finally crammed with information, much of it written in Greek to hide it from prying eyes, Zachary Macaulay was ready for the homeward journey to England. With joy he looked forward to the reunion with his family and friends after three long, arduous and eventful years in Sierra Leone.

Zachary discovered that many changes had taken place in his absence. His first and initial disappointment was to find that Thomas Babington and his wife Jean, Zachary's sister, had left Rothley Court in Leicestershire and were now living temporarily in Sidmouth on the south coast. Jean's health had been a constant problem and her physician had strongly advised her to spend at least a year benefiting from the sea air and a milder climate. And so to Sidmouth Zachary also went. The pleasant surroundings and the company of his friends proved a great benefit to his own shattered health as he gradually recovered his strength.

Yet he had loved Rothley Temple in Leicestershire. Within those walls God had met him and transformed him. Now he felt drawn by an overwhelming desire to return there for a few days. We can imagine him wandering through the empty rooms, recalling so much that had happened there to change his entire life. All that was good and noble for him had its genesis within those walls. 'To this place I owe myself,' he wrote, '...it would be hard for me to describe the variety of mixed emotions which I [felt] seated in the little parlour, of what has passed since I first entered its, to me, hallowed bounds'. Considering that Zachary Macaulay was a reserved Scotsman, one who seldom expressed his feelings, such words, with their depth of fervour, give a rare insight into the man.

Macaulay could not stay long at Rothley Temple musing on the past. Henry Thornton, William Wilberforce, Granville Sharp and others were anxious to see him and to learn in graphic detail all that had taken place in the last three years. A further surprise awaited him. In the past the inner core of men totally committed to the cause of abolition had met in various homes to discuss their hopes and plans: Yoxhall

Lodge in Staffordshire, Rothley Temple, and Wilberforce's home in Old Palace Yard, Westminster, were favourite locations. But in 1792 Henry Thornton had purchased a beautiful country home called Battersea Rise on Clapham Common. As we have seen, his father had bought property on the Common soon after his marriage and Henry had lived there as a child. Still a bachelor, Henry then invited his cousin William Wilberforce, also unmarried, to go and share Battersea Rise with him when he was not occupied with parliamentary business in the City.

Now swallowed up in Greater London, Clapham Common may not sound attractive, especially as we think of the bustle and noise of today's busy railway junction, but in the 1790s it provided a haven of quiet, a second home for overworked politicians and businessmen. Clapham was then a pleasant village some three miles from London, with its own community of about 2,000 and its parish church, Holy Trinity. Wealthier residents lived in large houses dotted around the Common. On the north side of the Common, Battersea Rise gave every appearance of a delightful English villa with wisteria covering its walls, intermingled with fragrant honeysuckle. Time-worn elms guarded the house, interspersed with tall tulip trees. Spacious lawns led on into fields with grazing sheep and nearby woodland.

Henry Thornton's vision did not stop at purchasing a country home for two bachelors. In the grounds of Battersea Rise he had two further houses built and offered them to men of similar convictions in the great quest for social improvement. Charles Grant (1746–1823), a former director of the East India Company, was one. He had made a fortune in the

Charles Grant

Indian silk trade and lived in godless luxury until, sobered and grieving after the death of his two younger children from smallpox, he found mercy and new life in Christ. Now all his goals and motivations were changed. Returning to England in 1790, Grant soon became a Member of Parliament, and one of the key supporters of the Sierra Leone Company.

Henry Thornton offered the other house to Edward Eliot, a close friend of both William Wilberforce and William Pitt. Together these three young men had once enjoyed many carefree, relaxing days, with Eliot eventually marrying Pitt's sister Harriot in 1785. When Harriot died in childbirth just a year later her broken-hearted husband, who had described himself as 'an infidel', at last found true consolation in Christ and recorded that God had used the sorrow 'gradually to draw me by it to a better mind'. Eliot, an influential Member of Parliament, now also shared the same concerns for social improvement, lobbying endlessly and passionately for them.

These four friends, Thornton, Eliot, Grant and Wilberforce, were the founder members of what became known as the Clapham Sect — a name first used in an article in *The Edinburgh Review* in 1844. However, it would be more accurate to call these pioneers of reform the Clapham Network — to coin a modern term — or even the Clapham Group, for only a few of the group actually lived on or near the Common. Nor were they members of any 'sect', in the correct sense of the word, but evangelical men, upholding historic Christianity.

Others whose names we have noted were also vitally associated with these four, drawn together in shared endeavour: men such as Thomas Gisborne, Thomas Babington, Granville Sharp, Thomas Clarkson and now Zachary Macaulay. Mainly Anglican in tradition, they followed directly in the footsteps of earlier eighteenth-century preachers such as William Romaine, Henry Venn, William Grimshaw and many others. Another strong attraction for these wealthy, generous and influential men was the ministry of John Venn, Rector of Holy Trinity Church, Clapham. The church had been rebuilt in 1775 at John Thornton's initiative and expense, and as soon as the previous incumbent died, Henry had invited John, son of Henry Venn of Huddersfield, to take up the position. Venn's twenty-one-year ministry formed a further centralizing point for these men of shared vision.

The lofty oval room or library of Battersea Rise was their customary meeting-place. Here they discussed their plans and future initiatives. Designed by William Pitt himself, the library scarcely gives the impression of comfort, and as an old illustration shows, was clearly a place where long debates took place, possibly chronicled by one of the wives, while others read or embroidered. As Zachary Macaulay was ushered into the library he would have glanced longingly at the bookshelves clothing every wall. His early love of reading had never left him, and his opportunities in the sparse accommodation in Sierra Leone had given him little opportunity for such pastimes.

For the moment, however, Zachary's pressing concern was to convince his friends that Sierra Leone was worth rebuilding for a second time. A vast sum of money had been lost in the destruction visited on the colony by the unruly French troops in those two short weeks. He feared his friends might think their resources better spent elsewhere. Even though Zachary described the bloodcurdling events that had taken place, the wanton sabotage and the fickle acts of looting and betrayal by some of the settlers themselves, he still managed to persuade the board of directors that it was well worth continuing with the Sierra Leone project as a homeland for freed slaves. It would prove to sceptics, he insisted, that Africans were indeed capable of commerce and industry and of running their own affairs.

The venture must go on, the board decided, and clearly Zachary Macaulay was the man to continue at the helm. But first they were anxious that he should meet a new friend of the Sect — the Clapham Network — a woman by the name of Hannah More.

7

MEETING SELINA MILLS

In the autumn of 1795 Zachary Macaulay met Hannah More for the first time. Understandably, he would have been apprehensive at the encounter, for he learnt that she had early hit the heights of literary success, had been acclaimed as one of the outstanding 'wits' of the day and been on terms of personal friendship with men such as Samuel Johnson of dictionary fame and David Garrick, the actor.

Born in 1745, Hannah was one of the five daughters of a Bristol school teacher, Jacob More, and his wife Mary. With little financial support, the girls were largely taught by their father until the older two, Mary at nineteen and Betty aged seventeen, began a small school for girls. In days when only the daughters of the privileged received much education, this was a risky venture. Soon they enrolled their remaining three sisters, Sally, Hannah, then aged thirteen, and the youngest, Patty, to be among their first pupils. The little school prospered, receiving local patronage, and before long had to move to larger premises as the younger More sisters graduated from being pupils to undertaking some of the teaching.

Hannah, the cleverest and brightest conversationalist among the sisters, had scribbled lines of verse from early years. Then she began to occupy her time writing plays for the girls in the school to perform. Life went on quietly enough until at the age of twenty-two she attracted the attentions of a local landowner, Edward Turner. Although he was twenty years Hannah's senior, they became engaged, and he was considered a worthy 'catch' by the other More sisters. Such a marriage would lift Hannah out of poverty for ever, and give her scope to develop her writing gifts. But for the next six years Turner kept postponing any wedding date. When at last one was named in 1773, the hopeful bride bought her trousseau and waited on the appointed day, together

Hannah More

with her sisters and guests, in the porch of Clifton Parish Church in Bristol. And still they waited. At last a message came from Turner that he wished to postpone the marriage yet again. Crushed and humiliated, Hannah broke off the engagement and for a period sank into understandable depression. However, the marriage-shy groom fixed an annuity of £200 a year on Hannah in compensation, a fact which enabled her to pursue her literary career.

When Hannah More first travelled to London in search of
sponsors for her literary work, she was entranced with the
sights and society of the big city. Together with her sister
Sally and youngest sister, Patty, she continued to pay annual
visits as she achieved her life ambition — an introduction
to some of the great literary men of London society, among
them Samuel Johnson and David Garrick. Both men were
entranced by the young Hannah More, filled with astonishment at her writing ability and attracted by her vivacious
personality. When Sally and Hannah told Samuel Johnson
that all five More sisters lived together, he exclaimed in astonishment: 'What! Five women live happily together! I love
you, all five. I will come to Bristol on purpose to see you!'

Above all, David Garrick, outstanding actor and playwright,
became Hannah's hero. On her annual visits to London she
often stayed with Garrick and his wife. His encouragement
inspired her and in 1777, four years after her first visit to
London, her most popular play, *Percy*, achieved astounding
success. But Hannah More was not happy. Standing on
the very pinnacle of renown, she realized the emptiness of
mere attainment, accompanied by adulation and eulogy.
In her dissatisfaction she found herself strangely drawn to
the writings of John Newton, vicar of St Mary Woolnoth.
Once a slave trader, but now a new man by the 'amazing
grace' of God, Newton's preaching and advice had already
influenced William Wilberforce and others of the Clapham
Sect. Wishing to hear him preach, Hannah attended St Mary
Woolnoth on a Sunday and later spoke freely and personally
to Newton of her inner need. In turn, as Hannah was
introduced to men such men as Wilberforce and Thornton,
her life perspective began changing. When David Garrick

died in 1779, the young woman was heartbroken; but in his death found that the last thread that bound her to the high life of London society had finally snapped.

From then on, and during the next few years, Hannah found true joy and satisfaction in fellowship with God and his people. Their aims became her aims as she now used her pen to promote social reform and mercy for the vulnerable and down-trodden. Without the magnetic pull of London high life, Hannah now spent much of her time writing at her home in Bristol. Her *Cheap Repository Tracts*, designed to bring religious and moral issues to the ordinary people in a popular and readable style, were hugely successful and marked the beginning of the Religious Tract Society.

In place of the bustle of town life, Hannah wished for nothing more than some quiet country cottage where she could retreat to write in peace, and also entertain her many London friends. Before long she was able to purchase Cowslip Green, a thatched cottage in the shadow of the Mendip Hills in Somerset. Then in 1789, at the age of forty-four, she decided to leave Bristol altogether and make this cottage her base. This she did for the next twelve years and at the same time also had a home built in Bath for use in the winter months when it was too cold to remain at the cottage. Here she had opportunity to attend Argyll Chapel under the evangelical ministry of William Jay. Patty More, to whom Hannah was particularly close, usually lived with her at Cowslip Green, often joined by their older sisters.

William Wilberforce, Henry Thornton, Thomas and Jean Babington and many others, including politicians and literary associates, found their way to the Mendips and enjoyed the delights of the rural surroundings — and in particular Hannah's company. Wilberforce encouraged Hannah and Patty to start small schools in the area for some of the poorest children and promised financial help from the Clapham funds to aid the endeavour. And it was to the home of these erudite and energetic middle-aged women that Zachary Macaulay was introduced.

An immediate rapport sprang up between the serious, single-minded Zachary, and the vivacious Hannah More. She quickly discovered his unusual mental ability and gift with his pen, and used him to assist in some of her writing work. A young woman, Selina Mills — first a pupil and then a teacher in the Bristol school — now lived with Hannah and her sisters. Gentle, even-tempered and compliant, Selina was almost like a sixth sister to the family and especially close to Patty. As one of Selina's tasks was to help Hannah by making fair copies of her work, nothing seemed more natural than to ask her to do the same for Zachary. Then the unexpected happened. Zachary fell deeply in love with this shy, beautiful twenty-eight-year-old. Now twenty-seven himself, he had written to his sister Jean shortly before his return from Sierra Leone earlier that year expressing his thoughts on marriage. In a moment of rare confidentiality, he had said: 'I hope on my return to England to find one name ... that will be sunk in mine, and whose possessor will be content for my sake to encounter even Africa's burning clime'. Could Selina Mills be that one?

But there were problems. Patty More had developed an intense and all-consuming affection for Selina, and with little regard for Selina herself had persuaded the younger woman not to marry. Zachary knew this and accepted the disruption it would cause in the More household if he showed any sign of his feelings. Displaying a stoic control, he thought he had succeeded, but had reckoned without the hawk-eyed Hannah More. She had apparently detected the situation, although Zachary himself still had no idea whether or not Selina returned his affections. With a few subtle questions, Hannah drew from Zachary some slight admission of his attraction and was determined to stamp on it in order to protect her sister Patty from distress. Unfortunately, she also promptly shared her concerns with Henry Thornton, who then cautioned Zachary on the matter. Upset at such a broken confidence, Zachary was even more determined to forget Selina Mills.

And that would have been the end of the story had not Hannah very strangely and insistently invited Zachary, together with Jean and Thomas Babington, to visit them in Bath shortly before Zachary was due to sail back to Sierra Leone early in February 1796. Having resolved to make no approach to Selina, Zachary agreed to a short visit, but also decided to clear the air with Hannah More. What had she actually told Thornton? Zachary wanted to know. How had his behaviour offended her? But she flatly refused to discuss the subject. Still Zachary persisted. At last she replied. Not only did the family regard a marriage to Selina as unsuitable, she assured Zachary, but Selina herself had no interest in him whatsoever, nor would she welcome any approach from him. Hannah's anxiety to protect her sister Patty, who could bear no rival to her affection, had led Hannah into a direct travesty of the truth. In addition to her concern for Patty,

Hannah was afraid that if the relationship were allowed to proceed Zachary would wish to take Selina back to Sierra Leone with him and that, in Hannah's mind, would spell almost certain early death in that malaria-ridden land.

For Zachary, that conversation with Hannah was the end of the matter. He believed what she said regarding Selina and later reported: 'It made me more resolute to make a painful sacrifice of feeling to what I thought was my duty.' He resolved not to give the young woman the slightest indication of his affection. Throughout the last dinner they all shared before Jean and Thomas Babington and Zachary left for London, Zachary did not even dare glance in Selina's direction in case he betrayed his feelings. Had he done so, he might have noticed that she too was struggling. When he left the house to board the carriage to London, Selina was nowhere to be seen — there must not even be a farewell, the sisters had determined. But as he walked towards the waiting carriage he glimpsed Selina through a window. Alone in the room, she was crying bitterly. Zachary's resolve vanished in a moment. Rushing back, he poured out all his feelings to the tearful Selina and, to his amazement, discovered they were fully returned. On the spot he proposed to her and she eagerly assented. Tearing himself away he hurried back to the carriage — an unexpected glance had changed his life.

The best part of an hour passed before Zachary could begin to tell Jean and Thomas what had happened in those few short minutes. From hopeless love and the prospect of further years of loneliness, he was left speechless with astonishment at how God had intervened on his behalf. Championing his cause, his sister and her husband agreed to return to Bath as soon as possible to plead with the More sisters for Zachary and Selina. But time was at a premium: Zachary was due to sail back to Sierra Leone in a fortnight.

The situation Jean and Thomas discovered in the More household on their return was ugly. Patty had suspected that something had happened between Selina and Zachary before he left. Questioning the girl with a vehement and cruel intensity, she had forced her to confess her affection. Although obliged to the More sisters and under their power, Selina held her ground. Yes, she did love Zachary, and she did wish to marry him. Jean Babington, with a good dose of the Macaulay forcefulness in her character, accused Hannah of dishonourable conduct and of lying to protect Patty. Despite Jean's words, Patty was unrepentant and when Zachary himself arrived back in Bath a few days later he found a stormy reception awaiting him. Instead of her usual warmth, Patty spoke to him with a 'repulsive coldness which quite surprised me'. Nor was Zachary entirely free from blame for the ensuing row. As none of the five sisters had married he expressed his surprise with cutting sarcasm that such fine women 'of intrinsic worth did not seem to possess that degree of estimation in the eyes of men which they merited'. It was a cruel barb, especially in the light of Hannah's sad experience with her engagement to Edward Turner. Zachary regretted his words the moment they were out of his mouth, but it was too late.

The scenes were so bitter that it became obvious that some compromise must be reached quickly. It is said that this single event brought the Clapham friends the nearest they ever came to outright dissension. In the end the young couple were forced to agree to two conditions as the only way to resolve the issue. Selina must agree never to accompany Zachary to Sierra Leone and could only marry if he remained in England, and secondly, the engagement was to be kept strictly secret — not even Selina's own family could know of it. Zachary was far from happy about such conditions. To insist that Selina should never go to Sierra Leone was quite wrong, and amounted to a predetermination of God's will for them. He felt that the More sisters had dealt shabbily with them. Selina herself knew she had no option other than to submit at least for the present.

After a final farewell, Zachary set off back to London. Only a few days remained before sailing. Stopping for the night on the way, he wrote his first letter to Selina — a letter full of devotion which ended with the words:

> It is now near midnight. May kind angels guard your bed; may God be your Father and Jesus your friend; and may you ever remain assured that no distance of time and place shall diminish the love I bear you.

God had intervened in a remarkable way for Zachary and though he must wait, he would leave for Sierra Leone once more with the joy of having gained the affections of the woman he loved.

8

ESTABLISHING
SIERRA LEONE

A raw wind whipped around the streets of Portsmouth, flinging salty spray into the faces of the waiting seamen. It was February 1796 and Zachary Macaulay had already been delayed a week waiting for a change in the weather to enable the captain of the *Calypso* to set sail for Sierra Leone. The port was teeming with sailors, travellers and crew, whose language and behaviour was frequently offensive and rude. He had little hope of any privacy. But despite all the distractions, Zachary's mind was preoccupied after the emotionally exhausting two weeks he had just experienced. A great deal of his time was spent pouring out his jumbled thoughts in letters to Selina. To console them both, Zachary shared with her lines of a hymn translated from the German by John Wesley:

> Give to the wind thy fears,
> hope and be undismayed.
> God hears thy sighs, he counts thy tears,
> he shall lift up thy head.

At times he felt angry at the treatment they had received from Hannah and Patty More: it was both unreasonable and unjust. He also feared that if God should wish him to remain in Africa then any prospect of marrying Selina must be abandoned. But as the days passed, calmer, more balanced and charitable thoughts filled his mind. Although he assured Selina that nothing in the whole world could compete with the love he had for her, yet he determined 'to sit so loose even to that object which is thus dear to me, as to be ready at God's will to give it up.' Even though circumstances were unpleasant in Portsmouth, Zachary did not resent the wait, for each new day brought another letter from Selina. But at last the wind direction changed and the *Calypso* was ready to set sail, but not before Zachary had one more opportunity to post a letter to Bath, assuring Selina that neither time nor place would alter his affections.

On board ship he met other problems. Some missionaries, hand-picked by Thomas Cole, John Wesley's director of the Methodist missionary work, were travelling to West Africa under Macaulay's supervision. About ten men and their wives were being sent by the directors of the Sierra Leone Company to evangelize among the African tribes. Macaulay had anticipated warm Christian fellowship with them on the voyage, but was sadly disappointed. Not only were most of the group quarrelsome and highly discontented, they were also filled with grandiose thoughts of their own worth and superiority. They expected gifts of land, cattle and money to be donated by the tribespeople to whom they were going, in thanks for their services. How could missionaries with such attitudes succeed in commending the gospel in the frequently difficult and fractious conditions of the African tribal villages?

On 18 March 1796 the *Calypso* docked in Sierra Leone and Zachary was touched by the crowd of faces — both black and white — all there to greet him after an absence of some eight months. But the first task that awaited him was to settle the would-be missionaries and, as he feared, many of them did not find Sierra Leone to their taste. All he could hear, so he told Henry Thornton, were 'doleful lamentations and bitter complaints'. They were surprised that Freetown did not resemble London or even Portsmouth, and certainly found no cake shops where they could buy treats such as gingerbread for their children! Zachary merely shook his head in dismay and told them that he had warned them of the conditions. Dissatisfied with the food and unaccustomed to the heat, most of them opted to go back to England. Just a few remained and became useful missionaries and fellow workers.

Security was an immediate priority for Macaulay after the fearful devastation caused by the invasion of the French peasant army, the sans-culottes, in 1794. To guard against a surprise attack in the future, Zachary had a government station built on a nearby hill, one he appropriately named Thornton Hill. Overlooking the town, it had a commanding view of the Sierra Leone River estuary. Gun emplacements pointing seawards were erected, ready to fire on any approaching enemy.

For further security, Macaulay planned to train these one-time slaves into a competent militia. This proved far from easy, for many of the settlers were timorous and unreliable. At the first indication of any danger they preferred to slip into the nearby forest with as many of their possessions as they could carry and wait until all appeared quiet again. But gradually, with a combination of lectures and encouragements, Macaulay developed an effective fighting force, making the colony more settled and safer than it had been formerly.

Zachary had his own house built in the cooler atmosphere of Thornton Hill and soon discovered the benefits of his new situation. During the years that followed he suffered less from the scourge of malaria and other tropical diseases than before and even found time for a little recreation, including horse-riding and occasional sea trips. Moving from the sweaty heat of the plain to the bracing air of the hill also lifted his somewhat morose spirit. He writes appreciatively to Selina:

> The air is certainly considerably cooler, particularly in the evenings and mornings, than at Freetown. The mountain is crowned with very deep and lofty woods, almost impervious to the sun's rays. Great numbers of monkeys and squirrels are everywhere to be seen. There are also deer and wild hogs in abundance. Within a quarter of a mile of my house there are no less than two very excellent streams of fresh water, one of which issues from a rock not above two or three hundred yards off.

Fresh from observing the schools that Hannah and Patty More were establishing in the villages around Cowslip Green, Macaulay decided to take a number of African children into his own home and teach them himself using the same system of rewards and incentives as the More sisters. In time he became deeply attached to these twenty-five to thirty children he was teaching and saw many of them respond to the Christian gospel as well as learn to read and write.

During his earlier period in Sierra Leone, Zachary had struggled to establish trade links with the surrounding tribes, or to develop much of the agricultural potential of the colony. One particular problem was the reluctance of the settlers to work the ground. That was a task for slaves, they maintained, and now that they were *free* men and women they saw no reason why they should undertake such menial labour. But gradually Macaulay and the staff of the colony reasoned, cajoled and showed by example what could be done. Before long the settlement began to grow its own rice — its staple food. Other crops were also successfully planted: coffee, ginger, tapioca, sugar, pepper and bananas.

Despite the easier circumstances, one thing, or more accurately, one person, was missing. He longed to see Selina and now his letters to her were slow and intermittent. Sometimes they had to go on the slave ships all the way to Barbados or Jamaica before being taken on the return route to England. In those preserved for us we can trace a growing tenderness and understanding between the two. Selina fears that Zachary may be downcast and longs to be able to cheer him. He assures her many times over of the depth of his affection:

> I have again sat down ... to tell you how deeply I love you and what a satisfaction it is to me to feel that though parted from each other so many hundred miles, yet being one in Christ we enjoy the privilege of meeting as often as we go into his presence. To this I owe many happy hours. I seldom

think of you without having my mind raised from earth to heaven… Thus, my dear Selina, you prove a help to me even here … and assist me to serve my God better, and to love him more.

Very few knew of Zachary and Selina's engagement, as they had been obliged to secrecy by Hannah and Patty More; but those who did, such as Thomas and Jean Babington, were quick to write to Zachary with warm descriptions of the one he loved. One letter from Thomas written after Selina had stayed with them in their Sidmouth home for over a month was glowing and complimentary. He had looked for faults, he admitted, but could find few. Added to her physical beauty, she was 'affectionate, candid [and] strikingly sincere'. Opinionated, she certainly was, Thomas added, but also ready to listen to the views of others and to change her mind if she saw she might be wrong. Above all, he noted her 'ardent desire to improve under the influence of the Holy Spirit'. Such a description must have brought real joy to Zachary.

The letters also provide some fascinating asides into the characters of various members of the Clapham Sect. As Selina met these friends on their visits to Hannah More's cottage, she formed her own judgements of their personalities and gifts, particularly comparing Henry Thornton with William Wilberforce. Zachary's reply is interesting:

In point of talents, doubtless there is a splendour about Wilberforce which quite eclipses the other [Thornton], but there is a soundness about Thornton's judgement and extreme considerateness… which serves as a counterbalance. Wilberforce's benevolence may be the more ardent … but

in the practice of self-denying duties Henry Thornton is his
superior. Wilberforce has stronger and more lively views
of the beauties of holiness and of the Saviour's love; but
Thornton has a more uniform and abiding impression of his
accountableness to God for every moment of his time and for
every word he utters.

The comparison continues, but the multi-sided aspects of godly character seen in different Christians is of interest.

At times Zachary had reason to be grateful that Selina had not accompanied him to Sierra Leone. Despite the improved circumstances, dangers still abounded. Sometimes slaves held in the depots awaiting transportation managed to escape and sought sanctuary in Freetown. Enraged, the slave trader would come storming up Thornton Hill to the government house and demand the return of his property. Technically he was in the right, for no law had yet been passed forbidding the trade. Should Macaulay return the desperate fugitives? Much depended on the circumstances. Bound by the laws of ownership and personal property, he often felt obliged to send the runaways back.

However, in some cases Zachary made an exception. When a mother and her three sons escaped from an African slave dealer known as 'Pa Wamba', Zachary rose to her defence. While he was obliged under British laws to uphold the Rights of Possession, he had explicitly come to Sierra Leone to champion down-trodden and wronged Africans. That a black man should be making money by selling his own people was especially heinous in his eyes. Pa Wamba was denied his demands and the small family set at liberty.

But above all, Zachary cared for the eternal destiny of the men and women for whom he had sacrificed the comforts of home and marriage. He was even concerned for the slave traders whose activities he had come to Sierra Leone to thwart. Describing one such encounter, Macaulay writes: 'He promised to read a Bible if I would send him one... He appeared ... much frightened and turned pale when I told him that last night's conversation [on the iniquities of the slave trade] might aggravate his punishment in the day of judgement.'

Stern, imperturbable and just, Zachary Macaulay managed Sierra Leone affairs with admirable skill. Certainly there were disgruntled settlers who disliked his even-handed decisions. Normally they either decided to forget their differences or left the colony for inland Africa, but on occasions they would hatch up plots against the governor. These were largely ineffective; but during 1798 an ugly situation arose when aggrieved settlers made common cause with one of the local chieftains, King Tirama. The king nursed a grudge against Macaulay because, in keeping with his policy towards black slave traders, Zachary had refused to return his runaway slaves. King Tirama's chance for revenge came when some irate settlers proposed a plot. First, the settlers planned to purchase arms from the colony's munitions, suggesting that they felt in need of this added security. Next, a group of Tirama's head men would visit Macaulay with some seemingly innocent request. If they found him unprotected and alone, they would murder him. Then, at a given signal, all the settlers who had purchased arms would run amok throughout the colony killing at random until they had eventually gained complete control.

By some means news of the plot leaked; and when twenty guns were unexpectedly purchased in a single day, Zachary knew that the situation was becoming serious and put the colony's own militia on alert in case of trouble. A surprise visit followed from some of King Tirama's henchmen. This confirmed his suspicions, and the plot failed. Still nervous, however, Macaulay slept with his loaded gun at his bedside for the next few months.

At last 1798 drew to a close, and as it did so Zachary Macaulay's hopes of his imminent return to England and to his Selina rose ever higher. One thing above all others concerned him in leaving Sierra Leone: the future of 'his' children, the thirty African boys and girls that he had been personally educating. These children were mainly the sons and daughters of influential local chieftains who wished them to have the advantages of a good education. Macaulay also had other motives. Following the failure of most western missionaries to make headway in West Africa, would it not be better for these children, many of whom were responding well to the Christian gospel, to become missionaries themselves one day and to evangelize their own people? So many westerners died of tropical diseases within months or even weeks of their arrival, but these children would be largely immune from such risks.

As Zachary was mulling over these things, an unexpected letter arrived from Robert Haldane, a wealthy young Scottish nobleman who had recently sold his ancestral family home and was seeking to use the vast sum of money it had realized to promote Christian missions in various parts of the world. Could Macaulay find about thirty children, Haldane asked, and bring them to Scotland to be taught and trained so that they could return as missionaries? Motivated by this amazing concurrence of thought, Zachary immediately set about gaining permission from the parents and making all necessary arrangements for the trip. But he laid down one proviso: he had grown to know and love these children and insisted to Haldane that he must have ultimate responsibility for their training and futures. At last all was ready and on 4 April 1799, having accomplished a further three years as governor of Sierra Leone, Macaulay (now thirty-one years of age) set sail with the children for England and Selina.

In the face of almost insuperable odds, Zachary had persevered and finally succeeded in settling Sierra Leone as an orderly colony. Freetown itself now had three hundred homes and a population of 1200 liberated African men and women and some European staff. Trade with surrounding tribes had been established, and the colony was becoming increasingly self-supporting. A young man by the name of Ludham had already settled into Freetown life in preparation for taking over from Macaulay. With a glad heart Zachary and his young charges sailed at last for England.

9

A MAN IN DEMAND

William Wilberforce, Henry Thornton and other members of the Clapham Sect were eagerly awaiting Zachary Macaulay's arrival. The situation was critical. After ten fruitless endeavours to steer a bill through Parliament banning the slave trade, they had at last hit on an expedient which at least partially met their demands. Henry Thornton had framed and presented the Slave Limitation Bill, a bill that proposed a ban on any slave trading from a substantial stretch of the West African coastline, so reducing the areas from which slaves could be purchased. On 12 April 1799 it had actually been passed by the House of Commons by fifty-nine votes to twenty-three. The Clapham friends were ecstatic. All that now remained was for the bill to be voted through the House of Lords. But as usual, the Lords played for time. They demanded 'witnesses' to appear before them to argue the merits of the case. And who better to undertake such a challenge than Zachary Macaulay with all the latest facts at his fingertips?

As Zachary's ship docked in Plymouth towards the end of April, he joyfully disembarked in order to make his way swiftly to London. He planned first to prepare for the accommodation of the African children who were still on board, taking the longer route round the coast and up the Thames estuary. Once that was done nothing must stop him from heading straight down to Bath to claim his fiancée, Selina.

Two other significant marriages had taken place among the Clapham group while Zachary had been away. In 1796 Henry Thornton had married Marianne Sykes and in 1797 William Wilberforce, who had now bought his own home, Broomfield, on Clapham Common, had lost his heart to the twenty-year-old Barbara Spooner. He proposed to her just one week after first meeting her, complaining that the beautiful young woman, seventeen years his junior, was filling his thoughts by day and his dreams at night. They married five weeks later. To Zachary it seemed that his friends had quickly forgotten their own experiences. Regardless of the fact that he had already waited three years to marry the woman he loved, these two happily married men merely assured him that he was needed in London and could not so much as visit Selina until the crisis regarding the Slave Limitation Bill had been satisfactorily settled.

We cannot be surprised if Zachary Macaulay lost his usual equilibrium and expressed annoyance at the delay. Added to this he was battling against yet another attack of malaria and felt more ready for his bed than for interrogation at the bar of the House of Lords. What would Selina think when she learnt that he had remained in London on business instead of coming down to see her? Penning an apologetic letter to his patient lover, Zachary wrote wearily: 'I have acted as I believe you would have advised me to act'. The days dragged past and it was not until 24 June 1799 that Macaulay finally took his stand as a witness in the House of Lords.

In the meantime, Zachary prepared for the African children to settle in Clapham village about a mile from the Common, and arranged for them all to be admitted to hospital to be inoculated against smallpox. This was a relatively new procedure at the time and fraught with dangers. Many of the children became seriously ill as a result, although all pulled through eventually. Meanwhile Zachary planned to set up a small school for them in Clapham, for he was apprehensive about sending his charges to far-off Scotland under guardians whom he did not know.

Much to the disappointment of the abolitionists, the House of Lords threw out the Slave Limitation Bill, using endless repetition, deliberate misunderstandings and irrelevant arguments to prolong the debate. For Wilberforce and his friends the result was particularly galling because they only lost by seven votes and later discovered that fourteen proxy votes, all in their favour, had been mislaid. Wilberforce confessed that he had 'never been so disappointed and grieved by any defeat'.

Now Macaulay could at last travel to Bath — or so he thought, until Wilberforce calmly informed him that he was still needed in London to assist with the drawing up of a Royal Charter for Sierra Leone. Exasperated, this time Zachary admits that he 'vented my feelings a little too strongly'.

'But I have promised Selina...' he protested. Thornton and
Wilberforce merely laughed and blamed him for being a
little too rash in making promises. Perhaps Wilberforce had
forgotten his own impatience to marry Barbara only a few
weeks after first meeting her. In fairness, Henry Thornton
did write to Selina inviting her to come and stay at Battersea
Rise; but extreme shyness held Selina back from venturing.

Finally, on 12 July, almost ten weeks after his arrival,
Zachary set out for Leicestershire and his well-loved
Rothley Temple, where Selina had also been invited by Jean
and Thomas Babington. Shy to a fault, Selina was never at
ease in the company of the powerful, wealthy and strong-
minded members of the Clapham Sect. Apart from Jean and
Thomas Babington, with whom she was entirely happy, she
usually managed to find excuses to prevent her from visiting
Battersea Rise. Rothley Temple, however, was an ideal place
for Zachary and Selina to meet again and before long final
arrangements for the marriage were in place.

On 26 August 1799, three and a half years after their
engagement, the long-suffering couple were finally married
in Bath. Zachary was thirty-one and Selina thirty-two. The
More sisters were invited for the occasion, but Patty had
maintained her opposition throughout this time and replied
suggesting that she never expected to see Selina again.
Regardless of the threat, Selina went especially to visit Patty
at Cowslip Green to placate the aggrieved woman, and at
last Patty and her sisters agreed to attend the wedding. After
the ceremony, when Zachary and Selina left for a few days
away together, we read that the sisters shut themselves up in
a room together where they could 'sob their fill'. Fortunately,

that appears to have been the last of their opposition to the inevitable union of Zachary and Selina and in the following years normal and happier bonds were re-established.

With Macaulay now appointed as secretary of the Sierra Leone Company on an annual salary of £400, it was imperative that he and Selina should live in London. Sensitive to his wife's shyness, Zachary decided to rent accommodation. Added to this, the strain of all the recent years of incessant toil in a tropical climate were beginning to tell. Zachary's health appeared to be crumbling. Deeply concerned, Henry Thornton arranged for him to be given the best medical help available. When a liver complaint was diagnosed, Thornton insisted that the newly-weds were sent off to Bath without further delay — much to the delight of Hannah and Patty More. Thornton even lent them a couple of horses so that they could enjoy rides together in the open country each day. The

James Stephen

therapy was successful and before long the Macaulays returned to London, where Zachary took up a colossal burden of work.

The following year yet another Clapham marriage took place — one of high significance for the future of the social reforms undertaken by the group. James Stephen, whose first wife had died four years earlier, wooed and won the widowed Sarah Wilberforce, William's sister. Stephen's own childhood and early life was erratic, immoral and sad. Like Zachary himself he had decided to emigrate to the Caribbean with his wife Nancy to start life afresh.

Settling in St Kitts, he practised as a lawyer specializing in overseeing British trade laws. Here he also witnessed slaves being treated with brutality and fearful injustice but, unlike Macaulay in Jamaica, he was stung with shame and determined to do all he could to stamp out the trade. While still in St Kitts he began feeding Wilberforce and the Clapham friends with vital information to provide additional evidence and argument for the parliamentary bills.

When his health began to suffer in 1794, James Stephen returned to England with Nancy and his family; but only two years later Nancy died in childbirth, leaving James with the care of their young children, including their newborn baby. In his grief, he often spoke to Wilberforce, who consistently and kindly pointed him to the Saviour, able to forgive his past, heal his sorrows and care for his future.

Now a new man by God's grace, James threw in his lot with the Clapham friends, using his fiery energies and acute legal mind to promote their aims. With Henry Thornton's glad consent, he and his family moved into the home built in the grounds of Battersea Rise formerly belonging to Edward Eliot, who had sadly died in 1797 at the young age of thirty-nine. Stephen was the perfect foil for Zachary Macaulay: vigorous, aggressive (he loved nothing better than duelling) and stormy, he balanced Macaulay's calm, steely, quiet poise. He was as dramatic as Zachary was cerebral.

Meanwhile, still far from well, Macaulay was facing unfair criticism over his attitude to missionary work. The Methodist societies who had chosen the missionaries to evangelize the inland African tribes in 1796, and had placed them under Macaulay's oversight, were highly annoyed that he had encouraged the least satisfactory among them to return home after only a few weeks. They accused him of caring little about world mission and the plight of the heathen and wrote angry letters demanding explanations. Zachary replied in a long and rambling diatribe covering sixteen foolscap sheets of paper. To take on a man like Macaulay in argument was a risky endeavour, as his correspondents would discover. He piled reason upon reason why a missionary who seeks to evangelize others must be beyond reproach, both morally and ethically. He had unhappily witnessed 'missionary efforts which in my opinion have done more real injury to the cause of Christianity than perhaps all the opposition of the enemies of missions', he claimed, adding with a venomous sting, 'I had the mortification of being witness to very reprehensible conduct on the part of the missionaries'. The least you can expect of a missionary is uprightness of character, he insisted.

The positive outcome of Macaulay's unfortunate experiences with these early missionaries was the founding of the Clapham Sect's own outreach, the Church Missionary Society. In April 1799, the new mission's ground rules were drawn up by Charles Simeon, incumbent of Trinity Church, Cambridge, together with John Venn, to whom the Clapham group looked for spiritual leadership. One of the fruits of the Evangelical Revival during the past century under the preaching of the Wesley brothers, George Whitefield and

others was a new awareness of the desperate spiritual
needs of the unevangelized world. This had led in 1792
to the founding of the Particular Baptist Society for the
Propagation of the Gospel among the Heathen. William
Carey, accompanied by John Thomas, sailed for India in
1793 with this organization. Three years later the London
Missionary Society, an interdenominational mission
commanding support from a wide spectrum of churches,
was formed. By creating yet another missionary society with
the Clapham friends at the helm, the group may be seen at
their most sectarian, for their undisguised aim was to export
an Anglican church system first to Sierra Leone and then
further into Africa, India and on into many other world
areas in an ever-widening sphere.

Still heavily involved in the affairs of Sierra Leone, Macaulay
was dismayed to hear of a violent outbreak against the
new young governor, Ludham. Described as gentle and
unassuming, Ludham was ill-suited to manage the often
disruptive elements among the settlers, who deeply resented
any form of authority. A core of settlers, mainly comprising
some who had come from Nova Scotia, were always on
the look-out for causes of dissatisfaction. They disliked the
judicial system set up by Macaulay, and wished to appoint
men of their own choosing to positions of authority. A yet
more contentious issue igniting their fury concerned their
demand to own the freehold of the land on which their
homes were built. Where Macaulay had been strong, even
inflexible at times, Ludham was 'mild and conciliatory'
in his dealings and scarcely two years after Macaulay had
sailed for England armed conflict broke out. Only the timely
help provided by the arrival in Sierra Leone of 500 ex-slaves

from Jamaica, complete with an armed guard, prevented the colony from descending into anarchy.

Those who comment on Zachary Macaulay's personality often complain of his rigidity, his sternness and his one-track mind. Certainly he was unbending and often stubborn, but he had changed vastly from the 'disagreeable, conceited youth with self-sufficient dogmatic manners' that had arrived from Jamaica little more than ten years earlier. One evidence of such a change was a humility of mind prepared to recognize his own faults, and even to ask his brother-in-law, Thomas Babington, for an assessment of the progress he had made as a Christian. With total candour Babington replied: 'Your chief faults, my dear Zachary, seem to me nearly connected with the natural ardour of your mind and firmness of character. These qualities are excellent when kept in due bounds, but their very excellence tends to relax the watch which should be kept over them...' He then added kindly, 'I think you have made considerable progress since you were last in England'.

Doubtless, Selina must have discovered that Zachary was not always an easy man to live with. Records of the times are dotted with references to his singleness of purpose, which could completely blot out all lesser matters apart from the one thing on which he was presently concentrating. Selina, on the other hand, was a retiring, home-loving, bookish woman; her total unselfishness and patience were remarkable, never more so than when the time approached for the birth of her first child.

Jean Babington noticed how frail the younger woman was looking and insisted on taking her away from London to the quiet of Rothley Temple for the final weeks of her pregnancy. Zachary himself knew that he had a number of engagements that would involve his absence from home and was relieved that his wife would be under the watchful care of his sister, Jean. Nevertheless, he was acutely aware of the approaching responsibilities of parenthood and urged Selina to join him in prayer for wisdom, and especially for grace to 'fortify our hearts against those temptations with which Satan may be apt to assail us' — the sin of parental pride.

His arrival at Rothley Temple a few days before the baby was due must have been a great comfort to Selina and on 25 October 1800 Thomas Babington Macaulay was born, named appropriately enough after the man who had so profoundly influenced Zachary's own life. As parents Selina and Zachary certainly had much to tempt them to pride in their first son, for this child would soon show evidences of a brilliant intellect and was destined to become far better known than his father as the great English historian and poet, Lord Macaulay. Even today visitors to Rothley Court Hotel will be proudly shown the Macaulay Room where little Tom Macaulay was born.

10

TOWARDS THE GOAL

With the dawn of the new century hopes for the abolition of the slave trade seemed as elusive as ever. During the 1790s the price of Caribbean sugar had been steadily rising, and no plantation owner was willing to see his profits eroded. Each bill presented to Parliament by William Wilberforce was thrown out either by the House of Commons or by the House of Lords. While William Pitt held office as prime minister — a position he had maintained for seventeen years — his close friendship with Wilberforce, an Independent MP, had been a distinct advantage to the aims of the Clapham Sect.

Then came a further setback. In 1802, Pitt resigned. The issue was the 'Irish question' — a grievance that had refused to go away, and the more so following an Irish rebellion in 1798. To Pitt the first answer was the establishment of a union between Britain and Ireland. On 1 January 1800 the Act of Union was passed, with the two countries formally united two years later. But difficulties arose with Pitt's proposal to extend the Irish franchise, allowing their elected representatives to sit in the English Parliament. In that way, he reasoned, any Irish problems could be handled and neutralized before trouble arose. But with Ireland widely regarded as the back door for French revolutionaries to attack England, Pitt's proposals divided his cabinet. An ill man in any case, Pitt resigned: he had had enough.

William Pitt the younger

The appointment of Henry Addington as the new prime minister was a further retrograde step for the abolitionist cause. A fervent supporter of the rights of plantation owners and of the trade that had made Britain prosperous, Addington was in no hurry to support abolition of the trade and even proposed extending it to further the development of the sugar trade.

Early in 1802 his government signed a peace treaty with Napoleon, hoping to bring an end to the revolutionary wars. But the peace between the two countries lasted only a year, and in 1803 hostilities broke out again, this time with Napoleon as head of the First French Empire — wars that would last on and off for the next twelve years. These issues all combined to prevent Wilberforce bringing yet another bill regarding the slave trade before Parliament, knowing that defeat would be almost inevitable.

Meanwhile, a host of new duties crowded Zachary Macaulay's calendar. Following the birth of little Tom Macaulay in October 1800, however, his father did take his only known

'holiday' during his entire life of incessant work. But it was
not a holiday of his choosing. A serious fall from his horse
resulted in a double fracture as Zachary broke both arms.
The severity of his injury was compounded by the fact that
as a boy he had suffered for five years from complications
after breaking his right arm. But two advantages sprang
from these few months of convalescence. First, he was able
to enjoy the early period of his new son's life together with
Selina, whose forbearance and unselfishness had often been
tested to the utmost. Added to this, his brother-in-law,
Thomas Babington, decided to contest a seat in Parliament to
represent Leicester in the forthcoming election. Zachary was
glad to be free to give his time and energies to campaigning
on Babington's behalf, helping him gain a seat that he held
for the next eighteen years.

Now officially appointed as a member of the Committee for
the Abolition of the Slave Trade, Macaulay combined these
new responsibilities with his duties as secretary of the Sierra
Leone Company. Even after William Dawes had become
governor of Sierra Leone once more, the affairs of the colony
were frequently in turmoil, making its oversight almost a full-
time job. One other responsibility remained that Zachary
could never forget: the progress of the black children whom
he had brought back to England to be educated. Supervising
the Society for the Education of Africans was added to
Macaulay's assignments — a brave endeavour, but one that
faltered in its earliest days, for regrettably all but five or
six of the Sierra Leone children died within their first few
years in England. Just as many English rapidly succumbed to
illnesses and died in West Africa, so these youngsters from
a tropical climate seemed unable to withstand the diseases
common in England. Most of the surviving children were

sent back to Sierra Leone to continue their education in their home environment.

As soon as Zachary had recovered sufficiently from his fractures he left Rothley Temple, together with Selina and the baby, returning to London to take up his many duties. A specially built home in the city, to be known as Sierra Leone House, was awaiting the family, with office accommodation attached. Birchin Lane was far enough away from Clapham to suit Selina but not too inconvenient for Zachary and seemed ideal.

Not many months had passed before Macaulay found himself heavily involved in yet another Clapham endeavour, one that would prove among his most time-consuming activities during the next fifteen years. What better way, thought the Clapham friends, to promote the reforms they were constantly advancing than a monthly magazine? They decided that the publication should be called *The Christian Observer*. An able editor was clearly needed. Josiah Pratt, assistant minister to Richard Cecil at St Johns in Bedford Row, took on the initial editorship, and the first issue appeared in January 1802. But Pratt soon found the work too onerous and so the responsibility was handed over to Zachary Macaulay. Remembering that this man had sight in only one eye, it was a costly commitment. But with his long-standing love of literature, a flair for creative writing and his astonishing ability to chronicle and collate material, he was clearly a good choice for the task.

These were days when the presses were spawning new periodicals, among them the *Monthly Review* and the *Critical Review*. Soon after *The Christian Observer* had been

launched, the highly acclaimed *Edinburgh Review* appeared
for the first time. But this Clapham periodical had a clearly
defined purpose. Above all it aimed to provide family-friendly
reading material, with articles that could be appreciated by
young people, but also included more penetrating matter
to counter the evils of the day. Strongly biased towards the
tenets of the Established Church, it was a direct challenge
to the *Leeds Mercury* — a journal representing the views of
Dissenters such as Baptists and Independents — with its
declared purpose of promoting Anglicanism as well as the
objectives of the Clapham Sect.

The new magazine was divided into five main sections. The
first contained biographical accounts of the great church
leaders of the past. Next came a 'miscellaneous' section
which could include articles on any topical subject, including
animal cruelty, field sports, secular news and even political
sketches. The third section was devoted to reviews of new
publications, which provided long, detailed analyses of the
works in question. One review, it was noted, extended to
twenty-five pages. Substantial and influential, they had the
power to make or break the book in question. Not surprisingly,
the next section contained *Reviews of Reviews*, providing
authors with the opportunity to strike back at comments
they felt to be mistaken or unfair. The last section of *The
Christian Observer* was an eclectic mix of articles describing
world events, recent discoveries, world exploration and
scientific inventions. The final pages contained lists of new
publications, both secular and religious.

The path of an editor is hard. He is blamed on every side:
some allege that he favours one position, while others
accuse him of promoting the exact opposite. In the case

of *The Christian Observer*, some complained that it was blatantly Calvinistic, while others declared that 'every sober evangelical Arminian will be satisfied'. Hannah More affirmed that it was valuable but boring, and Wilberforce backed up her opinion by complaining that it was heavy and lacked 'a little essential salt'. But the readership thought otherwise, and *The Christian Observer* gained a wide circulation and remained popular for well over half a century. Despite the barrage of criticism, Zachary carried on, usually getting up at four in the morning and spending the early hours of the day writing or editing articles.

With the increasing demands on his time, Zachary was finding that he was obliged to spend ever longer away from home. And he was concerned about Selina. She was lonely, and now with a second baby, born in February 1802 and also named Selina, her need of company and help was acute. Overcoming her shyness, his wife agreed at last to move to Clapham Common early in 1803, so making it easier for Zachary to spend more time at home and for Selina herself to have those around her to whom she could turn for help. A roomy comfortable house on the south side of the Common, known as the Pavement, was the family home for many years to come. Here Selina was happy to bring up her numerous family, for seven more little Macaulays were born in quick succession. Instead of crowded London streets, and the ever-present danger of highwaymen who robbed the unsuspecting, Selina had the delight of open countryside where the children could play in safety. Added to this, her family could enjoy the companionship of the other children of the Clapham friends, including the Thorntons, the four Wilberforce boys and James Stephen's large family.

With 1803 came new hostilities with France and her allies. England was in danger of imminent invasion with Napoleon determined to neutralize the power of the English navy before mounting a land assault. Nationalistic fervour was at its height, with all other issues pushed into the background. Reservists and even men with no military experience were rallying to the cause of their country. Zachary Macaulay himself headed up a company of Clapham Volunteers, parading the streets in battle array. All thoughts of the slave trade had to be temporarily shelved in the national emergency.

Not until 1804, after circumstances forced Addington to resign and William Pitt eventually returned to the helm, did the outlook for the abolitionist cause take on a more hopeful aspect. Although Wilberforce feared he could meet the same futile round of arguments against a further bill to outlaw the slave trade, he decided to try once again to force a vote through the Commons. With James Stephen, now on the Committee for the Abolition of the Slave Trade, using his powerful legal muscle behind the scenes, Wilberforce took courage. To his astonishment Parliament voted in favour of abolition on each reading of the bill and on the third and most crucial reading by 69 votes to 33. What had changed? Clearly the mindset of the country was shifting. Various reasons have been suggested: overproduction of sugar had caused the trade to slump; war had sharpened the moral conscience of the nation; but more significantly, revivals of true religion that were breaking out in a number of places had given birth to an ethical and spiritual tenderness among the people. On a practical level, a sizeable number of new Irish MPs had been introduced into the Commons. These men, for whom the cause of freedom was all-important, had voted in favour of abolishing the trade.

All that now remained was for the bill to pass through the Lords — success was in sight! But it was late in the Parliamentary season and Pitt persuaded Wilberforce to postpone taking the motion further until the following session. He argued that the peers did not like to be hurried. It was a fatal mistake. By the time Wilberforce re-introduced the bill in 1805 the pro-slavery party had packed the House, and Wilberforce, not suspecting defeat, was ill-prepared with his counter-arguments. The motion was lost by 77 votes to 70 — a crushing disappointment for the men of the Clapham Sect.

By this time the war against Napoleon and his allies had taken a turn for the worse for Britain, despite Horatio Nelson's conquests at sea and the spectacular triumph over the combined French and Spanish fleets at the Battle of Trafalgar in October 1805. After two major land defeats in October and December 1805, the situation looked bleak. It was too much for Pitt. Already a sick man, he died early in 1806. He had long suffered ill-health but the cause of his death seemed plain to Wilberforce: 'The love of his country burned in him ... and the accounts from the armies struck a death's blow within'.

To Zachary Macaulay fell the task of writing a suitable obituary to appear in *The Christian Observer*. It proved a hard task, for while he honoured Pitt's work and memory, he could not accept the smug Christian platitudes written about him — sentiments which he knew were patently un-true. But the loss of Pitt as an advocate of abolition seemed irreparable and was one which the Clapham friends all felt deeply. However, the fact remains that Pitt's support for the cause had been distinctly ambivalent at times, often taking second place to his own determination to remain in power. His death did not, in fact, spell the end of the hopes of the abolitionists, for the situation changed again when George III asked William Grenville, a member of the House of Lords, to form a new administration. A long-standing opponent of the slave trade, Grenville was determined to see the abolition battle to a conclusion and to remove this ugly stigma from British life. In his position as a member of the Upper House he was in a unique position to make sure that the Lords did not scupper the bill yet again when it came before them.

At the same time, Thomas Clarkson, whose early indefatigable labours had done so much to influence public opinion against the trade, became involved once more. Having suffered from exhaustion after his previous herculean efforts, he had been living quietly in the Lake District since 1794, but now emerged to take on the campaign with renewed vigour. He revisited many of his old haunts, whipping up public fervour against the iniquity of a trade that majored on the sale of fellow human beings. Urging his hearers to lobby their MPs relentlessly, he was encouraged as he recognized that the tide of opinion had changed. Where he had once met with abuse, he now discovered support.

Lord Grenville, in consultation with his Cabinet, decided on an unusual course of action with the next Abolition Bill. Instead of taking it through the various readings in the House of Commons before referring it to the House of Lords, he decided to present it first to the Upper House, hopefully gaining support there from the outset. This would prevent the tortuous delays and reversals so often experienced as their Lordships sought reasons to oppose the bills. On 4 February 1807, Grenville made a three-hour impassioned

Lord Grenville in the House of Commons

speech in the Upper House, lasting long into the night, using 'justice, humanity and sound policy' as his justification for soliciting their support. When the House eventually divided on the issue at five in the morning, the bill was passed by a resounding majority of 100 votes to 36. Victory was in sight.

23 February 1807 was a day of triumph and tears in the Commons — triumph because after seventeen long years Parliament at last voted by 283 to 16 to abolish the slave trade in the British Empire — and tears, especially for Wilberforce, as Parliament rose to congratulate him with resounding cheers for the outstanding success of his long campaign. He could only sit with bowed head, weeping for sheer joy and relief. Samuel Romilly, the Solicitor General, described the outcome of this vote in euphoric terms as 'the most glorious event, and the happiest for mankind, that has

ever taken place since human affairs have been recorded'. On 25 March George III gave his royal assent to the bill, enshrining it in the law of England.

Yet to give William Wilberforce sole credit for this final outcome would be misleading. Certainly he was the front man, and all the recent celebrations marking the 200th anniversary of the abolition of the slave trade have centred almost wholly upon his exertions, but many other strands of heroic endeavour contributed to this final moment. Thomas Clarkson's tireless efforts as he rode the length and breadth of the country were highly significant, as was the legal acumen of James Stephen and the financial backing of men like Henry Thornton. But last, and by no means least, was the hidden contribution of Zachary Macaulay. Always present in the gallery of the House of Commons whenever the subject of slavery was discussed, he prompted, reminded and suggested a host of relevant facts to boost the arguments of Wilberforce and others as they spoke. We read: 'His memory was so retentive that without the trouble of reference he could collate the papers of one session with those of three or four preceding years... Every friend to slavery well knew Macaulay to be his most dangerous foe.' He was, in fact, a walking encyclopaedia of facts and figures so essential for the back-up of Wilberforce's persuasive speeches. If in doubt of any detail, Wilberforce would say, 'Look it up in Macaulay', and know the answer would be ready to hand and accurate.

That night at Battersea Rise on 23 February 1807, Zachary, together with all the friends of abolition, rejoiced and thanked the God with whom all things are possible for the astonishing success of their cause.

11

ONE SINGLE AIM

Marriage to Zachary Macaulay was far from an easy assignment for someone of Selina's disposition. Gentle and retiring by nature, she knew that life among the Clapham group of friends and co-workers spelt the end to all privacy and solitude. Without prior appointment, members of the circle called at each other's homes, often bringing with them a crowd of other acquaintances. With simplicity and absence of any formality, hospitality was freely given — and expected. Doubtless to Zachary's disappointment, Selina's shyness made such a lack of any formal arrangements a constant problem. While other families went off on holiday together, visiting such friends as the Gisbornes at Yoxhall Lodge or the Babingtons at Rothley Temple, Selina would prefer to escape each summer with her ever-growing family to Barley Wood, the beautiful and substantial home that the More sisters had now built for themselves in the village of Wrington, in the heart of the Mendip Hills. There on the verandah, surrounded by honeysuckle and clematis, overlooking the rolling Mendips, she could bury herself in a book and read to her heart's content.

And the More sisters, especially Hannah and Patty, loved
her to come with her children. Young Tom Macaulay was
a great favourite with the elderly sisters. An astonishingly
precocious child, Tom provided an endless source of
interest. Contrary to popular myth that maintains he was
very late in talking, Tom had a great deal to say for himself
from the age of two — nor was it mere childish chatter, but
a stream of almost adult comments on life. The story is told
of the day the four-year-old, with his parents, was visiting
Lady Waldegrave at her Twickenham home, Strawberry
Hill. Hot coffee was accidentally spilt on Tom's legs. To Lady
Waldegrave, fussing apologetically around him, he simply
replied: 'Thank you, Madam, the agony has abated'.

Slight in build with a shock of fair hair, young Tom had a
phenomenal memory. Like Zachary himself, he could recall
vast chunks of material he had read and repeat it verbatim.
On one occasion he accompanied his father to some
appointment and while Zachary was deep in discussion, the
boy discovered a copy of Sir Walter Scott's newly published
ballad-style poem, *The Lay of the Last Minstrel*. As he waited
he read the poem through:

> The way was long, the wind was cold,
> The Minstrel was infirm and old;
> His wither'd cheek, and tresses gray,
> Seem'd to have known a better day...

Stanza after stanza he read until he had finished the long
poem. On his return home he sat down on his mother's bed
and repeated as much of the minstrel's adventures as his
long-suffering mother had time or patience to hear. Like his
father before him, the little boy was constantly buried in a

book, and would freely share the contents with all around, talking, as one maid recorded, 'in quite printed words'. Later in life he would maintain that if by some strange chance the whole of John Bunyan's *The Pilgrim's Progress* or even *Paradise Lost* by John Milton should disappear, he could supply the loss because he knew both works by heart.

The immediate challenge for Zachary and Selina was to nurture the talents of this intelligent boy without making him conceited, for Zachary recalled his own lifelong battle with pride as a result of undue praise heaped upon him as a child. Also they must remember that they had eight other children: Selina, Jane, Fanny, John, Hannah, Henry, Margaret and the youngest, Charles. The doting Miss Mores were a particular problem. Writing anxiously to Selina at Barley Wood, Zachary says,

> Let me entreat you to be on your guard in this particular and seriously to discourage by every possible means everything both in language and manner of those around you which may tend to exalt Tom in his own esteem.

Most of all, Selina and Zachary were concerned for the boy's spiritual state. When Tom started as a pupil at a boarding-school in Little Shelford, Cambridgeshire, at the age of thirteen Zachary wrote a letter full of fatherly concern and spiritual exhortation to his home-sick son:

> Think how much our blessed Saviour voluntarily and cheerfully bore for our sakes, to what pain and shame he was subjected, what sufferings he endured … and then you will feel your own afflictions light… Now, my dear Tom, I am

far from saying you ought not to feel keenly the separation for a few months from a mother who loves you so tenderly, from myself and from your brothers and sisters ... but pray to God, my dear Tom, that he would give you that calm fortitude and serenity of mind which is our duty to cultivate under all circumstances... Fix your eyes on that meek and patient Lamb of God whose life exhibits a striking example of self-denial and resignation and holy and cheerful obedience.

The years that followed the abolition of the slave trade were crammed with extra duties for Zachary Macaulay. Immediately after the Act was passed, the African Institution was formed, an organization designed to bring education, order, stability and trade to African society, starting with Sierra Leone and spreading further into the continent. Looking beyond Africa itself, the institution aimed at a universal abolition of the slave trade, for while countries such as France, Portugal and Spain continued the practice, gaping loopholes would remain for rogue British traders to persist, regardless of the law. With the Duke of Gloucester, son-in-law of George III, as president, the Board members of this new institution were largely made up of MPs and those who had been on the previous and now defunct Committee for the Abolition of the Slave Trade. Unanimously the new Board voted Zachary Macaulay himself to be honorary secretary. With Sierra Leone itself transferred from the responsibility of the Clapham Sect to the Crown, Zachary was relieved to relinquish the time-consuming oversight of the colony.

One of the clauses underpinning the 1807 Act set out the penalties to be exacted on any ship-owner caught transporting slaves to the colonies. Not only would his ship be confiscated, but he himself would be fined £100 for every slave discovered on board. One of the main tasks of the next few years for Zachary Macaulay was policing the Act, and bringing offenders to justice. In partnership with the dynamic James Stephen, Macaulay set about the task, and had the satisfaction of rescuing thousands of Africans from lives of degradation. Tragically, some ship-owners, fearing imminent capture, dumped their cargo of slaves into the sea and sailed on, rather than face the penalties. Other ship-owners thought of more subtle means of deception. Giving their ships French or Portuguese names, they sailed under bogus flags. When Macaulay discovered the *Commercio de Rio* docked in the Thames Estuary, with its obviously English captain boasting a Spanish name, with a full complement of handcuffs, shackles and padlocks on board, he knew he had a prize catch. With the Act constantly flouted, it became necessary to increase the severity of penalties. In 1811, James Stephen helped to draft a bill making slave trading a crime punishable with fourteen years transportation or five years hard labour.

Passions ran high among ex-slave traders. One man, ruined financially by the Slave Trade Act, suffered a period of imprisonment in Russia for debt. On his release he pushed his way angrily into the House of Commons and assassinated the prime minister of the day, Spencer Perceval, with a shot in the chest. In the face of such vitriolic fury, it is not surprising that Macaulay often found himself the target of irate and undeserved criticism, if not actual physical danger, as he used the pages of *The Christian Observer* to expose law-breakers.

Macaulay's position as honorary secretary of the African
Institution became redundant in 1812 when it too was taken
over by the Crown. Before he relinquished his secretarial
duties he received public and generous plaudits from the
government for his contribution, vigilance and exposure
of rogue ship-owners and traders. Such compliments were
double-edged in their effects, however, for Macaulay was
now revealed as the government's secret weapon, sabotaging
the schemes of these lawless men. At last they knew the
identity of their most dangerous opponent — that strange,
silent figure, always in the background taking copious notes
of all parliamentary proceedings. Outbursts of malicious
abuse filled the press. With character assassination their
primary tool, disgruntled ship-owners certainly knew how
to use it with deadly effect. Zachary was accused of lying
and deceit, and suffered endless venomous smears. Yet
despite it all, as Sir James Stephen, son of Zachary's friend
and co-protagonist James Stephen, later wrote: 'He drew on
himself the poisoned shafts ... and while feeling their sting
... never turned a single step aside from his path [in order]
to crush the slanderers'.

Having lost his salaried position as secretary of the Sierra
Leone Company in 1807, Macaulay was acutely aware that
he had a large family to provide for, and although Henry
Thornton and Wilberforce still supported him generously,
he decided to start a business, trading commodities such as
rice, maize, coffee and other goods between England, West
Africa and on into India. He also began buying up ships to
ply the trade routes between these countries, transporting
the merchandise. Nothing to which Zachary Macaulay gave
his hand was ever half done and before long business was

booming. Clearly he would need help, and so he turned to his nephew, Thomas Gisborne Babington, eldest son of Thomas and Jean. Under his uncle's guidance Tom Babington performed an excellent job, with the House of Macaulay and Babington now established in Sierra Leone. This thriving business not only met Macaulay's own family's needs, but gave him the opportunity to contribute generously to many of the great projects that he and the Clapham friends supported.

The Napoleonic Wars that had broken out in 1804 were still rumbling on throughout this time, bringing devastation, famine and death to the continent of Europe. Late in 1813 Napoleon bragged that his fixed purpose was 'to make all his enemies bite the dust.' 'He that sitteth in the heavens, I trust,' remarked Zachary prophetically in a letter to Hannah More, 'hears this vain boast with derision and will bring it to nought as he has done the former boasts of this impious man.' Scarcely a month later Bonaparte suffered a crushing defeat at the Battle of Leipzig in October 1813 — fearful casualties were sustained both by the Allies and the French coalition — the highest experienced in Europe prior to the outbreak of the First World War in 1914. Although Napoleon escaped from captivity on the Island of Elba to fight again, he was effectively beaten and his encounter with the Duke of Wellington at the Battle of Waterloo in June 1815 would prove his last.

War-weary, England exulted in her victory, and for Macaulay and his Clapham friends, the defeat of France gave them the opportunity to enforce the anti-slave trade laws on the French, aided by the victorious Duke of Wellington, a strong supporter of the abolition cause and warm admirer of Macaulay. At last the way also became clear to introduce the Slave Registration Bill, the brainchild of James Stephen. This bill was to prove the most effective weapon against the illegal slave trade. It required the personal details of every slave in the colonies to be recorded: sex, age, height, and all other relevant characteristics. From this point on it became far more difficult to smuggle any new slaves undetected into the colonies.

With Napoleon defeated, and the Registration Bill soon to become law, the stage was set for the grandest endeavour of Zachary Macaulay's entire life — the final abolition of slavery itself — a vision that he had never lost since his days in Sierra Leone. Neither his family life, his work on *The Christian Observer*, his flourishing business or any other concern could deflect him from that one great goal — to deliver African men and women from the shackles that had bound them for so many generations. Every nerve was tensed, every sinew strained to achieve that one objective. He was a man, Sir James Stephen records, 'possessed of one idea and animated by a master passion — a passion so benevolent that the coldest heart could not withhold some sympathy'.

12

THE GRAND ENDEAVOUR

An impossible dream. Not even the members of the Clapham Sect thought it feasible to abolish slavery itself in the present circumstances. Policing the Abolition of the Slave Trade Act had proved a mammoth undertaking in itself. What hope could they entertain of the grander project? Only one man thought differently. With true Scottish grit, Zachary Macaulay never took his eyes off the goal. To him this was a holy war, and a war he must win even if it cost him his health, friendships, fortune or whatever else he held dear.

With family circumstances gradually changing and their vital objective of abolishing the slave trade achieved, the Clapham friends had begun moving away from the Common to homes in other parts of London. Longing for a quieter life, William Wilberforce was the first to go. He sold both Broomfield on Clapham Common and his home in New Palace Yard, Westminster, in 1808 in order to buy a house in Kensington — still an unspoilt country area, yet within easy reach of Westminster. His hopes were misplaced, for his new home soon became the centre of attraction. James Stephen, married to Wilberforce's sister, also moved away, as did one or two others of the inner Clapham circle. By 1814 a much diminished circle remained on the Common, including few apart from the Macaulays and the Thorntons.

Then came dreadful news. In January 1815 Henry Thornton died. At only fifty-five years of age and with a family of nine children, all under the age of fifteen, his death was a severe loss. The centre and originator of the Clapham group of fellow reformers, he had been the financial and intellectual prime mover behind much of the Sect's endeavour. None outside his own family felt his loss more acutely than Macaulay. 'He was my polar star,' wrote Zachary to Henry's widow, Marianne, adding:

> A thought of him, of the gleam of his approbation, or of his graver look of doubt or dissent, mingled with almost all I said or did. 'What will Henry Thornton say?' was with me a question on all occasions ... I clung to his friendship and sought his society and now mourn his loss. Multitudes had benefited from his bounty ... but in my case I owe him almost all.

As if this bereavement were not enough, two more close friends died in the next three weeks. One was a gifted and godly young man of thirty-two, John Bowdler, on whom the Clapham friends placed great hopes for future leadership. Almost every issue of *The Christian Observer* that Macaulay produced contained one of Bowdler's fine, perceptive articles. But for Marianne Thornton this further death was an added blow, for Bowdler had been almost a son to her —

one to whom she would naturally have turned for support in the event of Henry's death.

Standing side by side with Zachary at Henry Thornton's grave was another close friend, the brilliant Dr Claudius Buchanan. Not long returned from India, where he had worked closely with William Carey, Buchanan had been involved in translations of the Scriptures into Indian languages. At forty-nine years of age, he had just completed a translation of the New Testament from a priceless and newly discovered ancient Syriac manuscript. Following the funeral Buchanan had stayed the night with Zachary and Selina, talking animatedly of the rewards he had experienced from the close study of the Scripture needed for such translation work. A week or two later he too was dead — a cold caught at the funeral had proved fatal. Clearly wondering who would be taken next, Hannah More wrote to Selina expressing her concern about Zachary's own health after three such grievous blows. 'He seems to be always working for others to the destruction of his own repose,' she warned.

Now aged fifty-five, William Wilberforce had been suffering indifferent health. Coupled with Henry Thornton's death, this clearly spelt changes in the leadership among the Clapham Sect. Thomas Babington was planning to give up his Leicester parliamentary seat; James Stephen had already resigned his parliamentary seat in frustration at the sluggish pace at which any changes were implemented. Thomas Gisborne was busy writing books on philosophy, moral ethics and geology. With no significant representative left in Parliament, only Zachary Macaulay, approaching fifty years of age himself, and James Stephen remained to carry the baton forward towards the ultimate goal: the total abolition of slavery.

Having sustained the intense workload of the editorship of *The Christian Observer* for fourteen years, Macaulay felt that the time had come for him to relinquish the time-consuming task. Throughout these years he had been the target of much brutal criticism — criticism which he had borne without becoming censorious. Now when Samuel Wilks, a competent successor, became willing to take on the work of the *Observer*, Macaulay resigned as editor in 1816, although he still continued to use its columns to keep the iniquity of slavery constantly before the readership.

Little remained to keep the Macaulay family at Clapham. All Zachary's immediate friends were either living elsewhere or had been taken in death. Tragically Marianne Thornton, Henry's widow, did not outlive her husband for long. In October 1815, only eight months after Henry, she died of tuberculosis, leaving her young family bereft of both parents. The need was only alleviated when a kindly couple moved into the family home, Battersea Rise, to care for the Thornton children. Meanwhile, with the pressures of his own business concerns in Sierra Leone and India growing ever more demanding, Zachary decided that it would be wise to move his family from Clapham Common to a home nearer the City and the Houses of Parliament.

In 1818 the family moved to a comfortable house in Cadogan Place, Kensington, not far from the Wilberforces and within easier reach of the City and of Downing Street, where Thomas and Jean Babington were now living. At the time of their move, Charles, the youngest of the nine Macaulay children, was five, while eighteen-year-old Tom had left home to begin his studies at Trinity College, Cambridge, sharing accommodation with Henry, the eldest of the Thornton children. Recognizing Tom's outstanding gifts, Zachary had given extra time and attention to every detail of the boy's education and social activities. At the same time he remained sparing in any praise lest Tom should become conceited.

From all contemporary references, the Macaulay children appear to have had warm affectionate relationships with each other and with their parents. When Tom gained the Chancellor's prize for a poem he had written in 1821, Zachary wrote to Hannah More describing the family celebrations on the occasion. 'You may imagine the ecstasy of his little sisters when they learnt the news. They were quite wild with joy.' Tom himself retained a deep appreciation of his home and an intense bond of affection with his mother, Selina. Each summer Selina had taken the family to Barley Wood, where the More sisters eagerly anticipated their visits. At last, when Hannah herself was almost seventy-five and her sisters increasingly frail, Zachary knew that it was impracticable to return each year and so bought a house in Brighton where the family could spend the summers. Apart from a few days here and there, he himself was rarely able to join them due to his many commitments and the causes he had taken up. Among these were the Society for the Suppression of Vice, and the Society for the Support and Encouragement of Sunday Schools. Added to this he frequently travelled abroad, most often to France to police French rogue slave traders.

However busy he was, Zachary still found time to write to Selina every day telling her about all he was doing. In Calais on one occasion, so he told her, a particularly bureaucratic French passport official, a 'sharp-looking fellow', had insisted on making a detailed report of Zachary's personal appearance. From this we have our best description of Zachary:

Aged 52 years, Height 1 metre 70 centimetres; brown hair, high forehead, brown eyebrows, grey-brown eyes, with a middling sized nose and mouth, a brown beard, round chin and oval face with an ordinary complexion.

Teasingly, Zachary adds to Selina, 'I really do not believe that if you had been put to it, though you have known me for twenty-four years, you could have given so accurate a description of me!'

As the months passed, it became acutely obvious to the remaining members of the Clapham Sect that little had changed in the actual circumstances of the slave population remaining on the British plantations in the Caribbean. The trade might be illegal, but fearsome cruelties were still perpetrated. Wilberforce had little stamina left to fight for further reforms: his strength was failing, his memory not as accurate as once it was, and family troubles were weighing him down. His would be only a supportive role in the last great fight to abolish slavery itself in the British dominions. Macaulay and Stephen both had fire and energy but were not MPs; there seemed to be no one who could replace Wilberforce as the parliamentary front man in the fight.

But in the purposes of God the right person emerged at the critical moment — Thomas Fowell Buxton, a committee member of the Africa Institution. Born in 1786, Buxton was thirty-five, married to the sister of Elizabeth Fry, the prison reformer. Recently elected as MP for Weymouth in Dorset, Buxton stood at the outset of his parliamentary career. Already he had gained a reputation for speaking out against issues of corruption and social injustice and was not only active in campaigning for prison reform, but was the earliest parliamentarian

Thomas Fowell Buxton

to crusade for the abolition of the death penalty — then in force for up to two hundred offences.

As he attended a committee meeting of the Africa Institution in 1821, Thomas Buxton surprised all the members by suddenly and vehemently speaking out against the Institution's lack of progress in relieving the sufferings of slaves on the sugar plantations. Fourteen years had passed, he declared, since the Act abolishing the slave trade, and although doubtless much had been achieved for Africa itself, little had changed for the slaves. Wilberforce listened in silent astonishment. Surely this was his man.

Almost immediately Wilberforce wrote to Buxton and asked him to take over the leadership in Parliament of all issues relating to the sufferings of the African peoples. Buxton hesitated. How could he undertake such an immense challenge? The months crept past. Still Buxton seemed undecided. At last, towards the end of 1822, Wilberforce, accompanied by Zachary Macaulay, travelled to Buxton's home in Cromer, Norfolk, to urge him to take up the challenge. But there was no need. Buxton had decided. This would be the grand object on which he was prepared to stake his entire parliamentary career, the aim of all his future efforts. Summoning other MPs of the same persuasion to Cromer, these dedicated men began to discuss tactics for their forthcoming campaign.

The first and most influential measure was Macaulay's own brainchild — the formation of another society, this time to be called the Anti-Slavery Society, specifically designed to work towards the total abolition of slavery itself. Not all were impressed with the idea. *The Christian Observer*, now edited by Samuel Wilks, later commented on reactions to this development: 'We can well remember that he [Macaulay] was looked upon for this as a visionary and wild enthusiast, even by some of his nearest friends'. Regardless of criticism, Macaulay pressed ahead, and Wilks could only admire his attitude, pointing to 'Mr Macaulay's great calmness of spirit' and his 'impartial judgement'.

The weeks and months that followed were crammed with activity. First the Anti-Slavery Society needed a new London office to house its undertakings. In addition Macaulay quickly realized that the most influential way to promote any fresh initiative was through the printed page. He therefore proposed the launch of a new publication — the *Anti-Slavery Reporter* — and agreed to be its editor.

This represented a huge burden of work by any standard, but for a man like Macaulay with sight in only one eye, the challenge was even greater. Not surprisingly it proved too much even for Macaulay's robust health and Wilberforce commented that his friend was shouldering a workload equal to that of at least four ordinary men. Early in 1823 Macaulay succumbed to a bout of serious illness, and was confined to his room for many weeks. As he gradually recovered, he found himself still suffering from weakness and exhaustion, so on his physician's advice he went to Leamington Spa to try out the energizing effect of the town's newly discovered medicinal waters. Increasingly it was obvious that at the age of fifty-seven, Zachary must decrease his work load.

But what could he relinquish? One thing only sprang to mind — his business — the House of Macaulay and Babington, established in Sierra Leone and now trading widely in Africa, Europe and India. His nephew, Tom Babington, eldest son of Thomas and Jean, had proved a competent business partner, and under Zachary's guidance had managed the day-to day affairs of the business satisfactorily, reaping the lion's share of the profits. Through Macaulay's skilful oversight the business had survived several financial crises which had rocked the City, and was now in a stable and profitable condition. Approaching Tom Babington, Zachary proposed making over the entire management of the business to him, with only one caveat — no major changes were to be made without consulting him.

For Selina and Zachary this would mean a large decrease in their income and a total change in lifestyle. So that their sons' education should not suffer, they must make stringent economies, and in 1823 the family moved from Cadogan Place into much cheaper accommodation in Great Ormond Street. Zachary gave up the use of his private carriage and reduced all his expenses as far as possible. With his indebtedness to Tom Babington's father, Zachary was inclined to view the young man in a charitable light and was prepared to trust him. He had no immediate cause to doubt that his nephew would handle the business well; he had done so in the past, and Zachary himself would always be close at hand if problems should arise. There is evidence, however, that Selina was not as sanguine about the arrangements as her husband. Her lifelong policy of unwavering support for Zachary in all his endeavours made her hesitate to say too much. She questioned the young man's judgement, but tried to stifle her fears. Perhaps she was wrong. Zachary must know what he was doing. Added to this, her own affection for Tom Babington whom she had known from his childhood made her reluctant to voice her opinion.

Meanwhile, Thomas Fowell Buxton opened his new anti-slavery campaign in April 1823. Rising in the House, he presented the sufferings of the slaves in words of passionate eloquence, doing all in his power to stir the consciences of his fellow MPs. Few could remain unaffected:

> The slave sees the mother of his children stripped naked and flogged unmercifully; he sees his children sent to market, to be sold at the best price they will fetch; he sees in himself not a man, but a thing — an implement of husbandry, a machine to produce sugar, a beast of burden!

In the face of formidable opposition from vested commercial interests, the knowledge that Zachary Macaulay and James Stephen were waiting in the wings to assist him, and the indefatigable Thomas Clarkson was ready as ever to travel the country on behalf of such a cause, gave Buxton complete confidence to present his proposal for reform with eloquence and verve. Stephen's acute legal brain and fiery personality spurred Buxton on while Macaulay's tireless research provided him with an arsenal of bullets to fire at the adversary.

Macaulay himself seemed to relish long evenings spent thumbing through daunting files packed with the facts and figures he had assembled and studying endless charts and statistics. All these he assimilated, stored with ease in his memory, or recorded in large folios to be reproduced at crucial moments for Buxton's use. And Buxton trusted Macaulay implicitly — he was seldom wrong. So much did he rely on this silent, serious man, that he called his private memoranda *My Macaulay*.

To these men it was immediately clear that the abolition of slavery would be a long-drawn-out process, and together they developed an eleven-point plan, one that would not immediately antagonize slave owners and yet would gradually work towards their ultimate objective. It included proposals such as: the immediate freedom of children born in slavery, a fairer hearing in the courts for the slaves, clear restrictions on punishments, a regulation of marriage laws, rest on Sundays and the facility to purchase their liberty. But as Buxton stated in his first anti-slavery motion in May 1823, his ultimate aim was 'nothing less than the extinction of slavery — in nothing less than the whole of the British dominions' — a grand endeavour but with many obstacles yet to conquer. It came as no surprise that the measures were defeated, and instead George Canning, Foreign Secretary and Leader of the House, proposed a wide-ranging motion asking for generally improved conditions for the slaves in British colonies. The motion was easily carried, but was too vague to be effective.

Next came a well-intentioned government move, but one that would prove disastrous. Selecting a single crown colony — Demerara — the Colonial Secretary ordered a ban on the flogging of women in that colony and prohibited the use of the cart whip to goad reluctant slaves. It seemed plausible enough, and even in line with the abolitionists' own proposals, but when Zachary heard the ruling he was dismayed. 'I held up both my hands in astonishment,' he reported. After his years of experience in Jamaica, he knew only too well that to ban the *whip alone* was synonymous in the minds of the slaves with freedom from slavery itself — it was the unwritten symbol of their bondage. The whip meant slavery. To ban it meant they were now free men and women, or so they assumed. Why then were they still required to toil long hours on the sugar plantations without pay? The predictable happened. On 13 August 1823 over 1000 Demerara slaves rose in revolt against their masters. If the British government had freed them, they were not slaves any longer. The crackdown was harsh; at least a hundred were killed, fifty more executed, and others sentenced to 1000 lashes — tantamount to a death sentence in itself. Opinion in Parliament hardened against any concept of abolition. The cause for which these men of the Clapham Sect had devoted all their energies received its most serious setback by this well-meaning but foolish gesture, with Parliament more reluctant than ever to listen to abolitionist pleas.

13

THROUGH TRIAL,

TOILS AND TEARS

Selina was right. She had never been fully happy with Zachary's arrangements giving their nephew Tom Babington sole conduct of the House of Macaulay and Babington. Two other men, both hand-picked and trained by Zachary, were running the business from the Sierra Leone end while Tom was in overall charge of all the orders, loans and sales. For three years Macaulay had heard little of the progress of the business, as he gave his sole attention to the accumulation of material to bolster the flagging anti-slavery campaign and to editing the *Anti-Slavery Reporter*.

The first whisper of trouble came from an indirect source. A certain Colonel Nichols, in charge of British troops on Ascension Island, visited Sierra Leone and was entertained at the House of Macaulay and Babington. He was horrified at the revelries, the excess of drink and the offensive behaviour which he witnessed there. Could Zachary Macaulay possibly know and approve of such things? He felt sure he could not. On reaching England he spoke to Zachary in private, telling him of all he had seen. Zachary was horrified and immediately called for Tom Babington, but found him strangely evasive and uncooperative. Without a moment's further delay, Macaulay sent for the head manager from Sierra Leone, demanding that he bring with him all the accounts and records of the firm's transactions.

Macaulay was sickened by what he discovered. Inflated with his own importance, young Tom Babington had entertained grandiose ideas of turning the firm into a vast business empire, but without any idea of how to balance purchases against sales or of the folly of borrowing huge sums of money without the means to repay. He had granted credit terms to unproven customers and had amassed large quantities of unsaleable goods, stockpiled in Sierra Leone. These alone, together with unsold properties, were estimated at over £100,000 — a massive sum for the day. Worse was to come. Babington had bought ships to transport material and built new factories on islands adjacent to Sierra Leone — all unpaid for. Wages for employees had been raised to five times the amount allowed by Macaulay — with the two trusted men in Sierra Leone turning a blind eye to the impending crisis, doubtless hoping for personal gain.

Quite clearly the young man had bankrupted his uncle in three short years. Zachary could get no explanation from him. Instead, Tom Babington locked himself in his bedroom, protesting that it upset him too much to talk about the situation. Why, for instance, Zachary wanted to know, had he lent considerable sums of money to a firm in Calcutta which was itself in a precarious position? Creditors were beginning to knock on Zachary's door, but still Tom refused to explain or answer.

Although Zachary was doubly embarrassed because of his close relationship with Tom's parents, their common disaster brought the two families yet closer if possible. A moving letter to Zachary from Tom's father has survived:

> *I am corresponding with Tom on this affair with you; but he is thrown into such a state that there is no hope of his doing anything... It is altogether a grievous affair, and falls heavily on an old man like me; but I look to my God for strength and holy affections. I have carefully abstained from all painful topics as much as possible in my letters to Tom. Poor fellow! His mind has been strangely thrown off its centre. Trials are good for us: may we feel this more and more!*

Meanwhile, Zachary gave himself unremittingly to trying to repair the damage his partner had caused by selling off property to pay outstanding bills. His sterling character shone out in his total unwillingness to castigate his erring nephew over his gross mishandling of the business. Realizing that Tom Babington could do nothing to help, he dissolved the partnership, releasing him from any further liability — but it left Zachary and Selina, with their large family, in a precarious situation financially. Over the next two years Macaulay managed to pay off most of the outstanding claims against the company, apart from money owing to members of the immediate family and friends. The Babington family estate in Rothley also suffered considerable loss as Thomas Babington tried to cover as many of the liabilities engendered by his son as possible. Eventually in

1830, at Selina's suggestion, Zachary asked their son Henry, now twenty-four, to go out to Sierra Leone and attempt to resolve the remaining chaos there. A fine young man, Henry gradually succeeded in sorting out the multiple aspects of the business, none of them free of debt, and closing them down one by one, until after several years the whole of the House of Macaulay and Babington had been wound up. So well did Henry conduct affairs in Sierra Leone and retrieve the family honour that he was offered a lucrative government position in the colony. With that income he was able to help support his parents in their need, and also his younger brother Charles, aged sixteen and soon to study at the newly created University of London. His sister Margaret, nearly eighteen, and Fanny, in her early twenties, also needed some support.

Perhaps alerted by their own financial disasters, Zachary and Selina were quick to pick up on a little local gossip when they visited their old friend Hannah More at Barley Wood in 1828. For many years Zachary had managed the elderly lady's financial affairs — dealings with her publishers, her royalties, her property, her staff and the many demands made on her money — all came under his eagle-eyed vigilance. Her affairs had cost him hours of labour as she became increasingly dependent with age. For five years she had patiently cared for her bedridden younger sister, Patty, who had died in 1825. Now, at the age of eighty-three, Hannah was oblivious to troubling circumstances affecting her reputation and honour that were developing within her own household. Rumour had it, so Zachary learnt, that her staff at Barley Wood were in the habit of 'night revelries in the village', bringing discredit on Hannah. Added to this, Zachary discovered that the manager of her estates was systematically robbing Hannah of profits due from her lands. With all his customary efficiency, Zachary investigated the situation and wrote a tactful letter to Hannah, warning her, earnestly hoping to save her from further embarrassment. You must sell Barley Wood, he urged, and move to a smaller property nearer friends in Clifton, Bristol. 'I am driven like Eve out of paradise,' wrote Hannah sadly as she heeded the warnings and left Barley Wood for the last time, but Zachary and Selina were right and their intervention meant that Hannah, who lived to be eighty-eight, spent her last years without financial anxiety.

Wilberforce himself had finally retired from politics in February 1825, leaving Thomas Fowell Buxton as the front parliamentarian to lead the battle against slavery. Meanwhile, Macaulay kept up his relentless campaigns through the printed page. Pamphlets, articles, and most of all the regular weekly issues of the *Anti-Slavery Reporter* came from his ready pen, gnawing away at the evil of allowing one man to buy another and use his 'possession' without any regard for humanity. Despite the setback of the Demerara rebellion, Zachary Macaulay and his fellow workers knew no such thing as defeat. We read in an early biography of Macaulay: 'For ten years he bullied the bullies; for ten years with sickening repetition [he campaigned] until frayed nerves could stand it no more'.

Cruel invectives were aimed at Macaulay, particularly by the *John Bull Magazine*, a weekly periodical started in 1820 by a certain Theodore Hook. Its editor railed against any whose views differed from his own, and Zachary Macaulay was a regular target. Accused of 'petty cheating and dishonest dealings', Macaulay was constantly vilified and all he did misrepresented. Determined to undermine the anti-slavery cause, Hook stooped as low as possible to blacken Macaulay's character, all veiled in a humour which delighted his readers. 'Saint Zechariah' was gaining much 'Zacharine matter' from West Indies sugar, he maintained, while accusing Macaulay of being a 'cunning Professor of Zachmackery'. At last, for the sake of the cause he represented, Macaulay was persuaded to issue writs for libel against the *John Bull Magazine* for defamation of character. It appears, however, that no proceedings were undertaken.

Although Buxton had succumbed to serious illness in the wake of the Demerara fiasco, he was soon actively promoting the cause once again, fed continually by Macaulay's steady stream of facts and figures to back up his statements. 'If the negro should be emancipated,' he once declared, 'he would be more indebted to Mr Macaulay than to any man living'. It is not surprising, therefore, that the destruction of Zachary's reputation and character was the aim of those bitterly opposed to the campaign.

Certainly Zachary had a one-track mind and was constitutionally unable to give himself to more than one major interest at a time. On occasions he became so silent, engrossed and immersed in his work that he paid little attention to anyone or anything else. Yet he loved his patient and long-suffering Selina dearly. Writing to her one morning in the stilted style of the day, he confesses:

> I got up about an hour and a half ago and have been praying
> that it would please God to continue you in health for many,

many years to come, for my sake, as long as he shall spare me and for my children after I am gone. Certainly I have cause to thank God that I have ever known you … I owe you much, and I owe him much who gave you to me. I have not indeed done all I might and ought to have done to promote your comfort — you have had much, I know, at times to bear with — and your patience and forbearance have often been tried…

Zachary's concern for Selina's well-being increased sharply when their second daughter, Jane, was suddenly taken ill and died in September 1830 — the first major breach in a family closely united and loving. Jane was only twenty-six and, although confident of her spiritual state, Zachary wrote sorrowfully to his son Tom, who had been unable to attend the funeral. He spoke of Selina's grief, for Jane was 'her mother's unceasing and affectionate associate, clinging to her with a fondness and devotion that has made [her death] more severely felt'.

Selina was not the only one to be deeply affected by the loss. Strangely inhibited in expressing his feelings, it would appear that this bereavement triggered a serious illness for Zachary himself. As usual he had buried himself in a mountain of work, perhaps to mask his grief, while also battling against increasing weakness. Early in 1831 he lost the fight, becoming so ill that his family despaired of his life. For weeks he was confined to his room, often delirious, with the sight in his one remaining eye becoming so inflamed that he was threatened with blindness. And all the time, his faithful Selina watched anxiously over him, while still mourning the loss of their daughter Jane.

Then came another tragic blow. Scarcely had Zachary turned the corner before Selina herself, exhausted and shattered in spirit, was taken ill. The main observable feature of her condition was a loss of interest in all around her, even in Zachary and the family. Something was seriously amiss, but her doctor made light of her condition, putting it down to the circumstances she had endured. He was wrong. With a surge of shock and anguish it became clear to the family that Selina was dying. It was so sudden, so unexpected. Three of their daughters who happened to be at home gathered round her bed and together with Zachary commended Selina's spirit to God. Then she appeared to drop into a sweet sleep. Zachary quietly left the room for a few moments. When he returned his beloved Selina had gone.

Communications were slow and the first Tom Macaulay heard of his mother's death was in a newspaper he happened to pick up. Devastated, he travelled home immediately, his outburst of grief overwhelming. Too ill himself to attend the funeral, Zachary was grateful that Tom was able to take charge. Gaining control over his own deep emotion, Tom provided an enormous support to a family reeling with shock.

Writing to Hannah More, Zachary penned the fullest account of all that Selina had meant to him:

> For thirty-two years we have been the sharers of each other's joys and sorrows and cares... Through a succession of years nine sons and daughters were given to increase our enjoyment ... and to form new links in the chain that bound us... With what unwearied resolution and self-denial

*her time and thoughts were devoted to the development
of their faculties and the dawn of those principles of piety,
truth, reverence, love and devotion in them.*

He continued by speaking of Jane, whom they had so
recently lost. The letter is long and sad, grieving over his
own deficiencies as a husband. Selina had 'fulfilled all my
expectations' and was 'all I could desire'. He spoke of the
way she had cheered and encouraged him through all his
labours, and willingly borne his preoccupations and many
absences from home. He describes her final weeks:

*The last month of her life was devoted almost exclusively
to the sick-chamber of her husband... She watched over his
every word ... His blindness, and his debility and his utter
helplessness for a time doubtless imposed upon her a degree
of exertion which may have laid the foundation of that
weakness which stole on her [so gradually that not until]
within a few hours of her flight to heaven was it discovered
to our grief and dismay that her strength was gone.*

At sixty-three Zachary's own strength seemed almost spent.
Vicious attacks of malaria over the years had undermined
his health, together with long hours of unremitting toil
from early morning until late at night. Aided only by a
flickering gas lamp, he had spent hours poring over rows of
figures, long after his family had gone to bed. It had taken
a heavy toll — especially on his already impaired eyesight.
And now, Selina, the woman he had loved and on whom
he had relied implicitly for thirty-two years had been taken
from him.

With Selina's death Zachary now entered a world desolate and changed beyond repair. On hearing the news, James Stephen wrote in deep sympathy:

> *My dear friend, In the morning and evening I think of you and pray for you... Be of good cheer, yet a little while and you will exchange these tears and conflicts for the unclouded light of God's countenance.*

He also wrote out of great anxiety for the future of their campaign. But clearly even he had underestimated Zachary Macaulay. He received an astonishing reply, almost a reprimand, written just two days before Selina's funeral — an occasion that his doctors had said he was too ill to attend.

> *Defeat I regard not. Let us do our duty and leave the issue to him who ordereth all events. If I were to admit your desponding views of our cause, I should sink into inaction. But because we have a difficult task in hand, are we to flag or show irresolution? Let us not yield for a moment to the temptation which would lead us to cease to strive... You dread failure. I have no such dread.*

Brave words indeed from a brave man.

14

THE FINAL TRIUMPH

Zachary Macaulay had been central to all the endeavours of the Anti-Slavery Society. What would happen to their 'Great Cause' if Zachary too were to die or be unable to continue his labours? Without his endeavours James Stephen and his co-workers feared the battle lost. Despite Zachary's brave words, his future looked fraught with difficulty. Bereft and facing loneliness and poverty, he had important decisions to make. His financial losses were such that he could no longer afford the family home in Great Ormond Street, itself modest in comparison with the previous homes he and Selina had shared. So now Zachary decided to move to a smaller house near Russell Square in London. With him went seventeen-year-old Charles and two of his daughters, Margaret, a stunningly beautiful girl, and Hannah, who would eventually marry Sir Charles Trevelyan. His other two daughters, the eldest, also called Selina, and Fanny, spent the next two years at Rothley Court with Thomas and Jean Babington, not far from their brother John, who had recently been ordained, and was responsible for a country church in Leicestershire.

Zachary would have been virtually destitute financially apart from the help of his eldest son Tom and of Henry, still living in Sierra Leone. Tom Macaulay was entering a career of glittering success as a writer and poet, and just the year before his mother's death had become MP for Calne in Wiltshire. His maiden speech, pleading the cause of the disadvantaged Jewish population, had taken the House by storm, showing he had imbibed much of his father's compassion for the downtrodden.

Perhaps one strand of hope that Macaulay kept in the back of his mind as he contemplated the future of the anti-slavery movement sprang from a situation he had begun to investigate some years earlier and which would be known as the 'Mauritius scandal'. It had all begun when Macaulay noticed a strange anomaly as he was compiling his endless lists of statistics: the male population on the island of Mauritius outnumbered the female by five to one. This could only mean that in spite of the hefty penalties against the slave trade thousands of African men were still being shipped to the island. Soon he was following up many different avenues of investigation and discovered that the population had virtually doubled since the island had been ceded to England from the French in 1810. Its sugar trade had 'unaccountably' increased fourfold in recent years, an evident mark of intensive slave activity. How could these things have happened? The answer was obvious — only by consistent and regular breaches of the laws forbidding the slave trade. Alerted to such violations, the Anti-Slavery Society swung into action and was soon hot on the trail.

Worse was to be revealed — far worse. As investigations continued, the most shocking cruelty was brought to light. Even to investigate such abuses could bring lethal vengeance on the heads of men like Buxton and Macaulay as they exposed unsavoury truths. Slaves were being flogged for the most minor offences; they were starved, dismembered, roasted alive, murdered at will by their overlords. Suicides were common; cases of mothers killing their own infants to save them from lives of merciless brutality, frequent. No matter how many slaves were wiped out either by suicide or murder, replacements from Madagascar and the Seychelles were swift and endless.

The effect of these revelations was traumatic. Thomas Fowell Buxton, himself a sensitive man, suffered a minor heart attack. The British public was outraged. The mindset of the people had already been elevated and purged by the effects of the powerful revivals of true religion that had been sweeping the country from north to south, from Yorkshire to Cornwall, over the last twenty years. Because Parliament constantly postponed any discussion of the issues raised by the Mauritius scandal despite the impassioned speeches of Tom Macaulay on behalf of the abused and exploited slaves, the Anti-Slavery Society called for public meetings throughout London and beyond to broadcast the appalling facts. The publicity created an outcry against such inhumanity and possibly did more than any other factor to bring about that final triumph that had seemed so elusive — the abolition of slavery itself.

In the meantime Zachary continued producing the *Anti-Slavery Reporter*. Boring and repetitive it might have been, but it gradually knocked down all the pro-slavery arguments. Then, with a boldness born of confidence in his cause, Macaulay published a booklet entitled *The Death Warrant of Negro Slavery throughout the British Dominions*. In it he dared to claim that imminent victory was in sight. With frightening intensity Macaulay listed all the evidences of forthcoming victory, mentioning in particular the Catholic vote, secured by the Catholic Relief Act in 1829 that had added 'the votes of seven millions to our ranks'. Bereavement, poverty and near blindness had not quenched this man's zealous spirit. George Stephen, another son of Macaulay's hot-tempered friend, James Stephen, reported that Macaulay had shaken off some of the calm composure of his earlier years and had 'assumed with age the ardour and fire of youth and with an impetuosity of impatience that startled even the young ... proclaimed that the day was won ere yet the battle was fought'.

Zachary Macaulay was right. Victory was in sight, but first the battle of parliamentary reform had to be fought and won. Significant changes had taken place in the country as a result of the Industrial Revolution, with its mass migration of people from the country to the towns. This sometimes left small hamlets represented in Parliament by two MPs while vast new conurbations like Manchester had no representation at all. The fight against prejudice and self-interest was fierce and long; two Reform Bills were rejected before the third, with the country teetering on the brink of revolution, was finally passed on 7 May 1832. The dominance and insistence of the Whig prime minister, Earl Grey, had won the day. At sixty-six Charles Grey remained a man of outstanding ability whom Tom Macaulay, writing later in life, could describe in words of undisguised admiration as 'the sole representative of a great age which has passed away'.

The Reform Act of 1832 was a vital precursor to that last grand fight of Zachary Macaulay's life: the total abolition of slavery. Under its terms fifty-six small boroughs were disenfranchised, the number of MPs in other lesser towns reduced from two to one and sixty-seven new constituencies created. Many who lost their seats in Parliament by the 1832 Act were hardened opponents of the anti-slavery movement. With the extension of the vote to a further 250,000 male householders (bringing the total franchise to 600,000, still only a fraction of the adult population) many new voters in favour of abolition now had an influence over who should represent them.

The pace towards abolition was quickening, but it needed careful handling. Rumours that they were soon to be free men and women had filtered through to the slave population in the Dominions, with riots breaking out in several places, most notably in Jamaica. These were crushed with customary brutality. Macaulay advised against pushing too hard for abolition before the political climate was right, but some of the younger members of the Anti-Slavery Society felt that things were moving far too slowly. Led by George Stephen, as fiery as his father, they formed a breakaway movement called the Agency Committee whose object

Medallion designed
by Josiah Wedgwood

was to travel throughout the country, raising the level of public protest to new heights. This, they maintained, would force the government's hand.

Using as a poster the evocative medallion designed by Josiah Wedgwood, renowned potter and friend of Thomas Clarkson, which depicted a slave in chains crying, 'Am I not a man and a brother', they travelled the country. In town hall and village tavern they gathered the crowds and gave public lectures, promoting the cause in which they so passionately believed. Macaulay was uncertain of the tactics and even found himself criticized for dragging his feet on the issue — a thing harder for him to bear in view of his lifetime of toils than the vitriolic and personal abuse he received from his opponents.

Round every street corner, displayed on many a wall and in shop windows, the posters showing the pleading slave met the eye of the public. The issue was now alive as the Agency Committee contacted candidates who were hoping to stand for the forthcoming general election in December 1832. They demanded that each one should support the abolition issue. They stirred up the newly enfranchised voters, urging them to elect only candidates committed to backing abolition. More than this, they published in the daily papers the stance of each prospective MP on the issue. Hopeful candidates began writing to the Agency Committee presenting their credentials: some claimed to have once met Zachary Macaulay, or others to have encouraged William Wilberforce in his endeavours. Thomas Fowell Buxton fully supported these efforts and even Zachary could comment wryly that voters were left without excuse and were 'now on their trial before the bar of the Most High'.

Ladies' Petition

FOR THE

Immediate Abolition OF

WEST INDIA

SLAVERY.

THE Petitions of the Female Inhabitants of Newcastle upon Tyne, Gateshead, and their Vicinities, for the immediate abolition of Slavery, after being signed by six thousand two hundred and eighty eight persons, were transmitted on Saturday Evening, to Lord Suffield and Mr. Buxton, to present to Parliament.

Newcastle upon Tyne, 13th May, 1833.

Notice following receipt of 6288 signatures

At long last, in May 1833, the bill proposing the abolition of slavery throughout the British Dominions was due to come before the House. No effort was spared in these last critical days. Buxton's daughter, Priscilla, secretary of the Female Anti-Slavery Society, set about gathering women's signatures to support the cause and soon received almost 300,000.

By the time the petitions were all pasted together on two enormous sheets of paper, it needed the Speaker and three others to carry them into the House. And still the petitions kept arriving until they numbered an estimated one and a half million. By the ceaseless lobbying of recent months, and the steady tireless campaigning of years, the nation had been roused to action at last. And behind it all were the powerful influences of the Spirit of God that had changed the personal lives and priorities of countless people throughout this period.

Back and forth swung the arguments in Parliament that May; sometimes the motion teetered on a knife's edge as amendments unacceptable to the abolitionists were introduced. These included freedom only for children, then a hefty compensation of £20 million to be given to slave owners for the loss of their labourers and a period of twelve years compulsory apprenticeship for former slaves (one that Buxton eventually managed to reduce to six) to ease the transitional period and prevent a flood of freed slaves roaming the colonies with nothing to do.

When the bill passed its first reading in the House on 14 May 1833, Macaulay contacted Wilberforce, who was in Bath, frail and probably dying, to tell him of the impending triumph of the cause for which both had expended their best years, and sending him details of the debate. With his usual accurate memory, Zachary wrote:

> This day ten years ago the abolition of slavery was first made a question in Parliament. Last night its death blow was struck. My dear friend, let me unite with you in thanks to God for this mercy.

But neither William Wilberforce nor Zachary Macaulay was able to witness that historical moment on 26 July 1833 when the Abolition of Slavery Bill passed its second reading in the House. Although Macaulay, usually present in the public gallery, was ill at the time, one new MP, a man destined to become a great British prime minister, William Gladstone, recognized his enormous achievements and could comment:

> There is a name ... closely associated with this struggle for the abolition of slavery, one who has been the unseen modest ally of Wilberforce, and the pillar of his strength; the name of that man is Zachary Macaulay.

When the dying Wilberforce heard of the success of the bill, he echoed Zachary's words with the memorable comment: 'Thank God, that I should have lived to witness a day in which England is willing to give twenty millions sterling for the abolition of Slavery'. Three days later, on 29 July, he died, leaving a society vastly improved by his own and his circle's endless endeavours. A year later a statue of Wilberforce was erected in Westminster Abbey with a long obituary, believed to be the wording of Zachary Macaulay. In it he said of his lifelong friend:

> His name will ever be specially identified with those exertions which by the blessing of GOD removed from England the guilt of the African slave trade and prepared the way for the abolition of slavery in every Colony of the empire ... He relied, not in vain, on GOD [whom] in his life and writings he had desired to glorify.

For Zachary himself only four years of life remained, and hard years they were. His eldest son, Tom, in whom so much of his interest and hopes had rested, and who by his impassioned eloquence as an MP for Calne had done much to promote the cause of abolition, received an appointment to be a member of the Supreme Council of India — a high honour indeed. But for Zachary it was a blow. He would probably never see Tom again, nor his daughter Hannah, who was going to accompany her brother to India.

They sailed in March 1834, and only a few months later, Margaret, Zachary's youngest daughter, recently married and with an infant daughter of her own, died after a virulent attack of scarlet fever. She was just twenty-two, beautiful and sweet-natured. 'The blow has been sudden and severe,' wrote Zachary to his eldest daughter, Selina.

Despite his grief he never doubted the mercy and kindness of God, and continued:

> She had all that the world can give her, and yet what is all that compared to one approving smile of her Saviour and an eternity in his presence?'

At the same time he had to admit:

> This is almost too much for feeble humanity, [but] may we be patient in the tribulation and rest in hope that those who sleep in Jesus are blessed beyond all conceptions of blessedness.

Shortly after Margaret's death fresh financial troubles beset Macaulay. The facts are scarce; but it would seem that old Thomas Babington's resources for meeting the vast debts incurred by his son's mishandling of the family business were exhausted. Money was owed to Wilberforce's estate and with

Babington unable to pay, Wilberforce's executors turned to Macaulay to meet the debt. Already impoverished, Zachary had no alternative but to sell his house. His youngest son, Charles, was pursuing medical studies in Paris and so, with his two remaining daughters, Selina and Fanny, Zachary moved to his son's flat in Paris. Selina, now thirty-two, was gentle and kindly like her mother, while Fanny was lively and cheerful. Together they did much to raise their father's spirits. Equally at home writing in French as in English, Macaulay soon began to contribute articles for the French equivalent of the Anti-Slavery Society. Not altogether sorry to leave the scenes of so much sorrow and harassment, Zachary spent much of the next two years of his life in France. Here he had many friends already, some among the aristocracy, who gladly welcomed the elderly campaigner into their homes. The slavery issue was not his only interest. Since his days in Sierra Leone, Macaulay had been concerned about the education of young children. His disappointment over his scheme to educate African children had not blunted the desire to improve such facilities, for these were the days when youngsters were employed for long hours in factories, coal mines and mills. Impressed with the French Infant School System, he wrote articles promoting similar approaches not only in England but in India and the colonies as well.

Comforted by letters from Tom, who wrote by every mail, he entered into the family celebrations when his daughter Hannah married Charles Trevelyan, who had a government post in Calcutta at the time. While Tom was occupied drawing up a legal system for the Indian sub-continent, and immersing himself in developing an educational programme for Indian schools with English as the primary language,

Charles Trevelyan was also involved in education and the improvement of living standards among the Indian peoples. Charles and Hannah's first child was born towards the end of 1835 and Tom could report to Zachary that 'she is the sweetest little child that I ever saw'.

In spite of such family support, Zachary was far from well. His sight was fast failing, with his strength unequal to the demands he attempted to place on his weakened body. His son Charles, to whom he was close, with Selina and Fanny, decided on one last possibility to help their elderly father. Perhaps the bracing mountain air of Switzerland would be beneficial. Towards the middle of 1836 they took Zachary to Geneva and were gratified to see the beauty and change revive his spirits, but it soon became evident that this was only a temporary improvement. Zachary Macaulay was evidently dying.

Thomas Babington Macaulay

A return to London seemed the best option. Here at least he could be among friends, and his daughters would have some support as they cared for their father. Charles accompanied them as they took a flat in Piccadilly. Weak and in pain, Zachary knew well he was dying and dictated his last will. With little money to leave, he wrote simply:

Since the former wills were made it has pleased the Almighty God in whose dispensation I desire with the most entire resignation and even thankfulness cheerfully to acquiesce greatly to reduce my property ... to a very uncertain amount. In the first place I desire with all humility and reverence to commend to the mercies of my God and Saviour the soul which he hath redeemed by his precious blood and in some feeble measure, I trust, restored to his image which sin had so miserably defaced and polluted. On his mercy alone I place all my hope that my transgressions may be pardoned.

At his death, he continued, he wanted no praise, no compliments, however much friends might wish to heap them on him. All such eulogy, he felt, would be 'wholly unmerited' and even 'a reproach to my sincerity'.

But one thing Zachary Macaulay did want as he lay in semi-blindness and pain — he wanted to see Tom again. An urgent request was sent to India that Tom, Hannah, her husband, Charles, and their young daughter should return as quickly as possible. But it appears that the ship on which they travelled, the *Lord Hungerford*, was slow and old and the months passed as it made its laborious way round the Cape of Good Hope and up the west coast of Africa. By May 1838 news came that the *Lord Hungerford* was nearly home. Zachary's hopes were raised.

Early that month Thomas Fowell Buxton visited his old friend and co-worker. 'God bless you and yours,' said the sick man as Buxton rose to go. 'Your visits are to me as water to a thirsty soul.' Others came and went. The Anti-Slavery Society meeting that month sent their founder a warm, if formal, acknowledgement of his invaluable services in the cause of abolition. And still Zachary waited and hoped. But the reunion was not to be. He died in the arms of his son Charles on 13 May 1838, at seventy years of age, taken at last to the land where the slave is free for ever, the blind can see, and all pain and sorrow have fled away.

When the *Lord Hungerford* eventually sailed into Dartmouth, Tom and Hannah were greeted by the news that they were just too late. Tom was heart-broken. Despite all his success and the human accolades heaped on him, his family meant far more to him. Hannah wrote sadly:

> My dear father whom I did so long to see was taken away just as I was pleasing myself with the thoughts of making known to him my husband and child. For our beloved father himself we can only say, 'Thank God that he is at last at rest; through much tribulation he has entered the kingdom of heaven. He has known of late years but little earthly happiness, but what does it all now signify except that he may now see the reason for the thorny path he was made to tread.

Although Macaulay had specifically requested no eulogies, glad acknowledgements of his services came pouring in. Words of profound appreciation, written by Sir James Stephen, son of Macaulay's friend and colleague in the *Edinburgh Review*, express the thoughts of many:

> That God had called him into being to wage war with this gigantic evil [slavery], became his immutable conviction. During forty successive years he was ever burdened with the thought. It was the subject of his visions by day and of his

dreams by night. To give them reality he laboured as men labour for the honours of a profession... The rising sun ever found him at his task ... His commerce, his studies, his friendships, his controversies, were all bent to the promotion of it ... In that service he sacrificed all that man may lawfully sacrifice — health, fortune, repose, favour and celebrity ... and he pursued the contest to the end. His memory will ever be dear to those who hate injustice.

In answer to popular demand for some monument to mark his tireless toils for the oppressed and needy, a pedestal was erected in Westminster Abbey not far from that of William

Wilberforce. Beneath a bust of Zachary, a fine likeness taken from an 1831 portrait, is a small copy of the Josiah Wedgwood medallion of the kneeling slave, followed by these words:

IN GRATEFUL REMEMBRANCE OF
ZACHARY MACAULAY,
WHO DURING A PROTRACTED LIFE, WITH AN
INTENSE BUT QUIET PERSEVERANCE
WHICH NO SUCCESS COULD RELAX,
NO REVERSE COULD SUBDUE
NO TOIL, PRIVATION, OR REPROACH COULD DAUNT,
DEVOTED
HIS TIME, TALENTS, FORTUNE,
AND ALL THE ENERGIES OF HIS MIND AND BODY
TO THE SERVICE OF
THE MOST INJURED AND HELPLESS OF MANKIND; AND
WHO
PARTOOK, FOR MORE THAN FORTY SUCCESSIVE YEARS
IN THE COUNSELS
AND IN THE LABOURS WHICH,
GUIDED AND BLEST BY GOD,
FIRST RESCUED THE BRITISH EMPIRE FROM THE GUILT
OF THE SLAVE TRADE;
AND FINALLY CONFERRED FREEDOM
ON EIGHT HUNDRED THOUSAND SLAVES;
THIS TABLET IS
ERECTED BY THOSE,
WHO DREW WISDOM FROM HIS MIND, AND A
LESSON FROM HIS LIFE,
AND WHO NOW HUMBLY REJOICE IN THE ASSURANCE,
THAT, THROUGH THE DIVINE REDEEMER,
THE FOUNDATION OF ALL HIS HOPES,
HE SHARES IN THE HAPPINESS OF THOSE
WHO REST FROM THEIR LABOURS,
AND WHOSE WORKS DO FOLLOW THEM.
HE WAS BORN AT INVERARY, N.B., ON THE 2ND MAY, 1768:
AND DIED IN LONDON, ON THE 13TH MAY, 1838.

Suggested

Further Reading

Booth, Charles, *Zachary Macaulay* (Longmans, Green & Co., 1934).

Cook, Paul E G, *The Clapham Sect* (Evangelical Library Bulletin, 1982).

Collingwood, Jeremy and Margaret, *Hannah More* (Lion Publishing, 1990).

Fay, Roger, *The Clapham Sect and the Abolition of Slavery* (Westminster Conference, *The Truth shall make you free*, 2007).

Furneaux, Robin, *William Wilberforce* (Regent College Publishing, 1974).

Hague, William, *William Wilberforce* (Harper Press, 2007).

Knutsford, Countess, ed., *Life and Letters of Zachary Macaulay* (Nabu Public Domain Reprints: first published, 1900).

Stott, Anne, *Hannah More: The First Victorian* (OUP, 2003).

Steven, Sir James, *Essays in Ecclesiastical Biography* (London, 1849).

Thomas, Geoffrey, *William Wilberforce and the Clapham Sect* (Westminster Conference, Out of Bondage, 1983).

Tomkins, Stephen, *William Wilberforce — a biography* (Lion Publishing, 2007).

Tomkins, Stephen, *The Clapham Sect* (Lion Hudson plc, 2010).